THINK SIMPLE
WIN BIG

How to Build the Business
of Your Dreams With a Few
Simple Goals

By Doug Bennett

ISBN: 9798462867910
Imprint: Independently published

This book is the 2nd edition of Doug's first book *Goals DO Come True*. Although many of the same ideas are shared in both works, Doug has applied many of the lessons in *Think Simple Win Big* to a newer, more niche audience of people who are either already small business owners, or are looking to become one.

This book was produced in collaboration with Write Business Results Limited. For more information on their business book, blog and podcast services, please visit www.writebusinessresults.com or contact the team via info@writebusinessresults.com.

Contents

Contents

Acknowledgements

This book is the essence I have distilled from continuous reading, courses, seminars, conferences, audio programs over the last 40 years, and the influences are great and many. I have added my "spin" or "take" on many ideas to make them my own. Wherever possible, credit is given where direct reference can be gleaned.

My greater MDRT family – if you are in the financial services industry and want to turn your life around, aim to qualify for MDRT, The Premier Association of Financial Professionals®. You will not regret it. There are so many people to thank, so if you are in MDRT and our paths have crossed and we shared a moment, lunch, dinner, a seminar, a beer or most importantly an idea, then I thank you!

Dan Sullivan and the Strategic Coach® Programme – especially Julie Cosgrave, for introducing me and gently nudging me along for I don't know how many years. I hope you finally got credit for me joining! If you didn't, then at least everyone who reads this book will know it's because of you that I joined the Programme. Although towards the end it was feeling like a rather expensive quarterly get-together (the result of my very low follow-through), there is so much I can track back to either receiving first-hand or being reminded of that has contributed to my success.

Paul Armson and Inspiring Advisers Online – Paul provides support for advisers to take their business from purely transactional to providing a tangible service. Paul provided me with the missing piece of the jigsaw for my business and gave me confidence to talk to clients with considerably more money. I was already confident in the £50,000–£200,000 space, but now I understand that, to quote Tony Gordon, "Bigger is not more complicated, bigger is just bigger", and I am confident with clients of all sizes.

Legends of Wisdom – Brian Tracy, Tom Hopkins, Jim Rohn, Jack Canfield, Norman Vincent Peale, Tony Gordon and Dale Carnegie, and the new kids on the block Simon Sinek and Tim Ferriss.

Finally, a big thanks to Georgia Kirke and the Write Business Results team for helping me to bring this book to life.

Dedication

My mum, Lucy Bennett – stolen from my brother Jim's tattoo, "Your strength will guide me always."

My team – thanks for everything you do to make me look great. Full training will be given! (they will know what I mean).

My sons, Jason and Jake – you make me so very proud!

Bonnie – many promises have been made throughout our time together, I can now finally come good on all of them. Just let me have the revised job list and the order you want them completed in. I love you.

Dedication

Foreword

I first met Doug at a life insurance convention in Birmingham in 1997. I say met; we didn't actually speak but we were both addressing the two-thousand-strong crowd at the same time, which I imagine counts as "met" on some level.

Years would pass before I actually got to know Doug, which was really down to reading the first edition of this book, *Goals DO Come True*. It was a small book but packed with useful insights that I have used to great effect ever since.

The book prompted me to contact Doug and tell him about the positive effect that it had had on me. I asked him to let me know if he ever published another book as I would love to read it. As a result, I was privileged to receive a copy of the manuscript of the new edition and I am delighted to say that Doug has excelled himself for a second time.

I thoroughly enjoyed his candour and his self-effacing style of writing; it was a book that made me feel that I had made a new friend or become reacquainted with an old one.

I kept the manuscript, which was covered in my yellow highlighter, as I had found so many useful pieces of advice contained within it that I felt that I really needed to go back over the book and re-read all of the great advice it espoused.

But it was much more than that! I knew Doug was a successful businessman, but it was only by reading his book that I truly got to know the man, the struggles, the mindset and, ultimately, the success that only comes to someone who has truly managed to master their mindset – and Doug most definitely has.

There is so much in this book that it could easily be referred to as a blueprint for success because it covers so many things that many books in this genre fail to cover. It's the many little things that Doug covers that truly add up to a successful life and career.

Doug talks eloquently about his passion for coaching and mentoring and the great value that a coach or mentor can have in our lives. He even went on to become a formidable coach and mentor in his own right, as can clearly be seen in "Sarah's Story"; and I know that hers is just one of many success stories as Doug has been a profound influence in the lives of many, just as he has been in mine.

One thing that jumps out at me from the pages of this revealing and often uplifting book is the many unsaid things that show Doug's true character and essence, and that is that Doug cares. I am not sure if he is truly aware of just how much this one thing has played in his success, but I can tell you without reservation that anyone who cares "first", regardless of what they may obtain from their relationship, will invariably find a level of success that eludes most people, and there is a very good reason for that.

People have a sixth sense when it comes to another person's intent, and Doug's success in his field clearly shows that the overwhelming majority of his clients have sensed his high level of integrity from the outset and have granted him their absolute trust. This has allowed Doug to become recognised as one of the top one percent of the world's greatest salespeople.

The very first book I ever read after entering the world of life insurance was *How I Raised Myself from Failure to Success in Selling* by Frank Bettger. I don't remember much about the book as I was just twenty-two years of age at the time, but this one line from the book went on to change my life forever. The line read:

"I resolved right then to dedicate the rest of my selling career to this principle: Finding out what people want, and helping them get it. I can't begin to tell you the new kind of courage and enthusiasm this gave me."

It is most definitely true, and I believe that either knowingly or unknowingly, Doug has lived by this powerful philosophy, and hundreds if not thousands of people have been the grateful beneficiaries of a man who truly walks his talk and always puts the interests of others before his own.

And that is the true overriding secret of not just Doug's success, but anyone who wants to follow in his footsteps.

Mark Anthony Baker (The Belief Doctor)

Author of *An Unbreakable Spirit* and *The Imprint Phenomenon*

Foreword

Introduction

The inspiration for this book came from a list of goals that I'd written years ago and forgotten about. I rewrote my goals over the years with an occasional date. My first set of goals was written in 2004 and included completing the London Marathon, which I achieved in 2005. When I found this list of goals in 2012, I was amazed to see that I'd achieved nearly all of them.

These goals were related to my business and my personal life. As we go through the book, I'll share some of them with you and give you advice on how I achieved them. Sometimes I didn't even realise that what I was doing at the time was leading me towards another of my goals. But looking back I've realised how everything connects.

My journey isn't a linear one. I've had success and failure along the way. In fact, just a decade ago I was on the edge of bankruptcy and now I'm a millionaire. Consistently setting goals has been instrumental in helping me get to where I am today, with a successful business, a healthy bank balance and, most importantly, a happy marriage.

There are also certain core values that I believe are essential in business. If you cultivate these, you'll not only find that you are happier in yourself, but also that you develop a loyal client base who will stay with you through thick and thin.

Throughout the book I talk about my wonderful wife, Bonnie. I've written this from a personal perspective, so wherever you see the word "wife", feel free to interpret this as husband/

spouse/significant other – whatever term you choose.

If you're just starting out in the world of business, the advice I provide in this book will certainly help you set off on your journey on the right foot. If you already have a business, I hope that this book will help reinvigorate your passion for your work and give you some useful advice that improves your business' performance, whether you're currently doing well or have hit a rough patch.

More than anything, I hope that this book helps you to create a happy and balanced life. Working hard is all well and good, but if it's to the detriment of your personal life, then what's the point? I hope that sharing my journey and some of the mistakes that I've made along the way will help you to avoid a few of the same traps and give you a smoother path to success.

I have more than 30 years of experience in running a successful financial services business. I've had professional triumphs and faced professional challenges. I've been through some very challenging personal times too. However, I've come out the other side with a smile on my face and I'm happy to say that I've achieved the success I always wanted. I'm proof that goals do come true, so join me as we explore what you can do to make sure your goals come true too.

Chapter 1: What Is an Entrepreneur?

A quick reality check

Wouldn't it be great if we could have a business idea that we're passionate about, quit our job and then call ourselves a successful entrepreneur? It would be fantastic, but at that point you are not an entrepreneur. You're on the path but the journey is only just beginning.

Whilst I hope to inspire and encourage you and help you stay motivated, it's important you don't get over-excited by the word entrepreneur. First, you need to set up good foundations based on integrity and expertise, and offer a valuable service that people are willing to pay for.

There has to be a degree of experience and you've got to start making a living from something, and then you've got to start employing people (if that's your business model); so now, all of a sudden, you're offering greater value to the world and profiting from it. Now you're an entrepreneur.

If you have 17 different ideas and you move on each one but none of them is generating an income for you, then you are not an entrepreneur.

You have to be realistic about things. Yes, you can get enthused and excited and that will carry you over hurdles and the obstacles you might face, and you do need to have that passion to carry you through, but if you are looking for business longevity, there's no such thing as get rich quick. It's more of a get rich slow.

Overnight success

Of course there are exceptions to that rule, especially now with so much reality TV. People are propelled out and into social media fame and some of them go on to make a lot of money. But they might be only two or three people out of 1,000. Statistically, you are more likely to be one of the other 997 or 998.

Even if you think someone has been an overnight success, chances are they're 28 years old and not 18, which also probably means they've put in ten or more years of hard work to get to where they are now. There will have been times when the money was lean or they were rejected, or they just failed miserably and had to start again from scratch. It's better to keep your focus on you and the journey you are on.

What you need to really get going and become an entrepreneur is to bring all of you to your idea. For example, you might not be the only coach, mentor or graphic designer, but you will be the only one who can do it like you.

Be you

No two business owners think and act in an identical way. Think of three people you know who are in the same industry, are they the same? I'm a bit of a cheeky chap and I can get away with that with my clients because of who and how I am. But if I wrote down a couple of sentences and asked someone else in the same industry as me to use them with their clients, they just wouldn't work. You are your unique selling point and that's what you need to remember.

You might see someone else and feel inspired by what they are offering. Perhaps they look as though they have a really successful business model, but their model won't work for you because you're not them. Plus, it's important to remember that you can't be 100% certain that their business model is really successful. You don't know what you don't know, and you can't see what you can't see.

You could go onto the Companies House website and have a look at their turnover or wade through the business owner's social media, but that might not show you the big picture; and the big picture might be that the face of the business has a team of 27 staff making them look brilliant, and that another strand of their business is the actual earner. You can't always tell.

If that person has been in business for a while and you're just starting out, you can't instantly emulate their success because you won't know what's taken them to where they are; and what they've needed to do to get there might be out of alignment with your values. Being an entrepreneur isn't just about starting up a new business and making money. It's a huge journey in personal development and you'll get to meet parts of yourself you have never met before.

Keep it simple

Keep it simple. If you felt called to leave your job and set up your own business, what was the reason for that? If it was because you wanted to do things differently, to do things your way, then why would you start up on your own and try to copy someone else? It's time to build what's unique and authentic to you. If you start a new business going against your own values, there's every chance you would have been just as happy in your old job because at least then the income was guaranteed. You'll never make money from a business you don't fully believe in. You won't want to commit to your business if it's not sitting right with you and aligned to your values.

When you copy someone else your heart isn't in it and

you'll likely end up one of those here-today-gone-tomorrow startups. This is why it's helpful to have peer support, coaches and mentors, but all of them need to be there to help you bring out more of you. We will explore this in a later chapter. It's good to feel inspired by other businesses but you need to come up with your own version of any of those offerings. Copying will only make you miserable and more prone to giving up in the long run.

If you are looking for inspiration and support to build your business, there will be an association or peer support available for whatever industry you are in. It's a good place to begin, and remember that even if you are openly sharing ideas, no one can steal your idea because they cannot possibly deliver it in the way that you can, nor can they attract the clients who would want to work with you because, as I have already explained, you are your own unique selling point.

When you create in line with your own values and work with integrity, you'll find your business has longevity, and in turn this increases trust in your clients. I have the same mobile phone number now as I did in 1990. A client with a business card from 30 years ago can dial the number on that card and it's still me who answers.

If you're just doing things for your own benefit, as opposed to helping everybody to win, then you will end up exhausted and run out of opportunities quickly. You'll lose trust and end up losing credibility in an industry you are really passionate about.

You'll find happiness in business when you create something that is unique to you. Nobody else can compete with that because, remember, they're not you. You must start here.

Chapter 2: No Diving Allowed

Start with a trip to the beach

I'd like you to imagine that you're visiting the beach for the very first time. You're sitting on the sand, listening to the waves crashing onto the beach, enjoying the sunshine. Because it's really sunny, you keep applying suntan lotion throughout the day. At some point you feel as though you need to cool off. Remember that this is your first time at the beach. So, you walk down to the sea and you have a paddle. The water washes over your toes, laps up to your ankles, maybe you even wade out until you're knee-deep.

As you get used to being in the sea, your confidence increases. You walk in a little deeper, with the water reaching your waist, up to your elbows and eventually your chest. Then, you're swimming. At this point, some people get bitten by the bug for the ocean. They love being in the sea and their confidence increases. Those people might buy a mask, snorkel and fins and go snorkelling. They start to see the fish underwater, all the wildlife that lives on the sand. It's exciting, but it's a bit more risky than paddling or swimming.

Then there are people who love what they see from the surface so much that they decide to go scuba diving. They have an air cylinder on their back and all the gear that allows them to go deeper. They have a totally different view, but there's more pressure and there's more risk than bobbing along at the surface.

Finally, you have the people who go all out. They go deeper and deeper, wearing all kinds of technical equipment and specialist suits to take them to the bottom of the ocean.

What does going to the beach and scuba diving have to do with starting out in business? I'm going to show you how this analogy applies, and why that matters to you as a new and excited entrepreneur.

At the beach

If you're sitting on the beach just watching the ocean, you're not risking anything and it's a relatively safe place to be. You might play around with a few business ideas in your mind, and that's a lot like regularly applying suntan lotion to prevent getting sunburn.

The problem is that if you sit in the sun for too long, you're going to get sunburn even if you apply lotion. And in a business sense, if you sit around for too long with your ideas, you'll probably burn them out. You can't only create a business in your head. It's better to start taking some action, even if it's a small action, and that involves more than just sitting on the beach.

Getting into the sea

When you are ready to dip your toe into the ocean of possibility, you might begin with some market research; you're beginning to get a feel for this experience in a low-risk way.

Perhaps you're working on your business alongside keeping your regular job, or you're working from your kitchen table and not incurring extra expense. As you get more confident you might begin to test the market by letting prospective clients know about the service that you are offering. That's the equivalent of going for a swim.

You could then continue to fine-tune the services you offer, or move into a deeper niche. Now you're snorkelling. You might decide you want to work with a select and elite group of people and go full out into the world as the face of your new business (or take out a business loan). Now you're entering scuba diving territory which some people might say is volatile and risky, but if you've enjoyed looking at the ocean, paddling, swimming and snorkelling, you've done your market research and built a stronger set of muscles.

No diving allowed

So why no diving from the get-go? Some of you might feel ready to dive right in, but most of you would be better off sitting on the beach first and getting to know the terrain. It's wise to scope out what you might need for this journey, what it costs, and find the right entry point for you so that you don't face major risk before you are prepared. Perhaps you set yourself some goals to be met before you go snorkelling, and you should definitely be able to swim before you even consider scuba diving.

There's also no pressure for you to reach the level of scuba diving. Perhaps your goal is only to paddle or swim. If all you ever need to do to achieve all of your life and business goals is to go swimming, then swim. There's no need for you to have the added risk of snorkelling or scuba diving if you don't need it to be happy.

Remember the lifeguard

What I want you to remember is that you don't need to rush into the sea and, secondly, you don't need to go into the sea alone.

It's a good idea to have a lifeguard on the beach, someone who knows the terrain and can watch over you as you start to paddle. Maybe the lifeguard will go in with you if that's what you need to feel confident taking the next step.

It's really useful to have a lifeguard watching over you in case you get a bit out of your depth and start struggling, or if you don't understand how the tides work and are a little unsure of how things will work out. For my clients I'm the lifeguard, there to hold out a helping hand and make sure they're ok. I'm also there to rescue them in case they become a bit overconfident and get swept out to sea.

That's my role as the business owner: to watch over my clients' progress, to make sure they're taking sensible risks and to keep them safe if they push things a little too far, or coax them out a little further if they're inhibiting their own progress. And having a lifeguard to watch over you (like a coach or mentor) will keep you safe and stop you from making costly (potentially life- or business-threatening) mistakes. After all, once you've seen the beauty of the ocean, the chances are you'll want to snorkel or scuba dive more than once!

When is the best time to start out with a new business venture?

Firstly, you should make sure you're in the position where you have three months' worth of money to cover whatever your monthly bills are, as well as your food. Don't forget about your food – it's all well and good covering all of your bills, but if you can't afford to eat, you'll be dead! Let's take an average couple in the UK who may earn circa £40,000–£60,000 per annum. Having this three months' worth of money set aside means that if you lose your job or your income dries up, you have a bit of cash to tide you over and you don't need to grab for the first thing that comes along.

Once you've saved that figure of three months' worth of money, look to double it. That will give you six months' worth of money, which for most people will be between £10,000 and £15,000. That can sit in your bank or premium bonds and act as your emergency fund. When you have this amount of money available, you can start to think about investing. But the vast majority of people don't have anywhere near that amount of money in their bank or building society as an emergency fund.

If you don't have that much saved up in your account, but are thinking about diving into a business venture or something riskier, my advice to you is to stay on the beach a little bit longer to build up your confidence, increase your reserve funds, and limit stress levels.

Remember that sometimes you can achieve your goals without taking anywhere near the amount of risk that you think you need to take. Very often, it's a case of being consistent. In fact, I'd say that saving consistently over a longer period and steadily expanding your comfort zone will get you a better return than being very, very risky.

Being a financial adviser by trade means I am always assessing risk versus reward, and whichever type of business you are in will require you to do the same. The higher the level of risk, potentially the higher the level of reward; but equally the higher the level of risk, the higher the potential for negative consequences.

As an entrepreneur, you will need to explore your own financial comfort levels with everything, from website spend to marketing budgets. All of this comes with its own risk and you need to establish what you can tolerate. Some people only want to be in the black and won't tolerate going into the red financially, but as an entrepreneur you also need to remember you are looking at long-term gain and sometimes you need to take a risk to reap the reward.

It's up to you to decide your risk tolerance based on your financial starting point and your end goal, but there's no need to rush into deep-sea diving. Spend time paddling, learning to swim and becoming really proficient before you dive in deep.

If you would like any extra help with building a solid plan to help you navigate these waters, feel free to head over to my website using the QR code below and get in touch with me about how we can work together.

Chapter 3: Impostor Syndrome

That voice inside your head

It's really important to be aware as you progress to the diving or scuba diving stage of your business that there's every likelihood a voice inside your head will tell you that you're not up to it: "Who do you think you are to go scuba diving? You'd be a whole lot better off sitting on that beach gazing out at the sea and just wondering." That inner voice is doing its best to keep you safe, but at times it's just spoiling all the fun and adventure. It's holding you back.

We all have this voice and, while its intentions are good, you'll do well not to listen to it. There will be times when you need to push way beyond it to achieve your goals.

I have this voice, this inner critic. It grows as you grow. As a child, it may have told you that you'd never be able to ride a bike or drive a car, but now you can, and you don't doubt that fact. Now that voice will tell you that you're not capable of earning £30k or £80k, or making your first million. The trick is to keep growing beyond the voice.

I'm in an incredibly different place now to where I was 15–20 years ago. There has often been a voice in my head challenging each progressive step. It's demanding. "Who do you think you are to do that, loser? What makes you think you deserve this success? If you do it, you'll fail and people will find out you're not as good as they thought you were." We all have this inner critic and, if we want to drive our business to become the very best it can be, we need to push beyond it.

I still have challenges because I keep growing and growing my business. I work with a mindset coach now because that supports me at the highest level. There is no such thing as impossible, but we need to overcome the impostor syndrome to move towards this belief that we can achieve anything we want. If you stay within your comfort zone, the place where your inner critic is silent, you'll be stuck.

The phone call

One phone call was all it took for me to reach a seriously big business goal. If I'd given in to the inner critic, the impostor syndrome, nothing would have changed. It's worth mentioning here that this phone call didn't make me an overnight success; that came because of all the hard work I'd put in.

The nature of the financial services industry means that there are a number of compliance service networks always looking to recruit new advisers. If I was happy with where I was, I'd usually dodge this type of call or get off the phone as quickly as possible, but this day was different.

It was different because I'd found myself in a situation where the network I was with had just announced it was no longer interested in representing in the wealth arena, and was just going to concentrate on mortgage and protection advisers. Its focus had shifted. I was faced with having to find a new network. During this one phone call and the invitation to join a new network, I realised I could reach my goal of earning £500k if I signed as one of their representatives.

Just before Christmas 2019 I hit my £500k goal, and then

another half a million pounds just after. That's what my goal was, and in those two years, that's what happened, with ease.

Of course, I did the due diligence because I wasn't going to do anything that would negatively impact my clients. It was a win-win and it felt right, so I took the opportunity.

I could only make that move in direct proportion to my developing mindset. If I'd tried to go from £25k to £500k, the chances are I would have said no to that phone call because it was too big a jump and my negative inner voice (the one prioritising safety and playing small) would have talked me out of it. We'll talk more about goal setting in Chapter 5.

Mindset muscle

You have to build your strength, build the mindset muscle, and you need external support to do that, otherwise you can't see the wood for the trees. This inner critic becomes a lot more vocal as you expand your comfort zone, and you have to know that this is all that it is, it's not the truth. Sometimes you even have evidence to prove that you can do something, but this part of you, this outdated self-image of what you're capable of, tries to dictate your decisions.

Dan Sullivan of Strategic Coach® explains that we each have Unique Ability®, and for this reason it's vital to find your own business path and not try to recreate someone else's.

There are billions of people on the planet and none of us are the same. Each of us is unique. Often you cannot see your own Unique Ability®; it takes an outside person to tell you what it is. You might view another person as amazing and vice versa, but you don't necessarily see your own brilliance.

A good way to explore what your Unique Ability® might be is to send a note out to 20 or 30 people and ask them to write a few words about you. You're most likely to receive lots of similar words and phrases about yourself, but if someone else repeated the same process with the same people, they are unlikely to get the same answers. There might be a couple of similarities but the responses will not all be the same; all of a sudden it will be obvious that you and this other person are different.

When I did this exercise it became obvious that one of my Unique Abilities® is being calm. When my friends or clients experience a lot of stress and they feel like they're really up against it, I calmly help them sort it all out in one way or another. Because I am authentic, people naturally feel comfortable around me. I'm the same Doug out in the world as I am in private behind closed doors, which helps me a lot in business.

When you know what your Unique Abilities® are, you can start to get rid of all the stuff you're not really good at, or that you don't like doing, and you will end up with three or four things that you are absolutely amazing at. Knowing what your Unique Abilities® are gives you a choice.

You can decide to start doing those things that give you pleasure, and start looking at ways to outsource the rest. For example, once you know what it is that you excel at, you can effectively delegate anything that isn't your Unique Ability®. You can increase your work-life balance by bringing more of your Unique Ability® into the world.

When you realise that no one else can do what you do in the way that you do it, impostor syndrome becomes a lot less significant; only you can be you and work in the way that you do. You are infinitely more capable of achieving great things, way more than you might ever believe.

At some point in your business you will have an idea and your mind might say you're not up to it. It's your job to check in, to see if your idea is in keeping with your Unique Ability®, to make sure that that idea would take you forward in the direction you want to go and, if so, tune out the voice of the inner critic. It may be there to protect us from danger, but you do not have to believe what it says.

A lot of these "I can't do this or that" thoughts were planted in our minds when we were very young. We might never know the source, but we do need to move beyond them.

Some of these thoughts are easy to identify: "You aren't educated enough, you bunked off school, you can't paint", and so on.

Any sentence that begins with "You can't" is one to watch; lose the apostrophe and the letter t and you pivot to "You can."

YOU CAN!

If you want to drive your business forward, you need to constantly review your goals. Make them achievable but also demanding of personal and business growth. If they seem impossible to reach, your impostor syndrome and that voice will go crazy. Set your goals just beyond arm's length, so that when you give a good stretch you can reach them.

You can't always see the inner critic clearly, which is why striving to develop your mind and be supported by (and accountable to) a coach or mentor is invaluable. You need to feed your mind and tip the balance of your thoughts firmly towards the positive. Don't let the lies of the inner critic block your success. Learn to discern thought from truth, and grow beyond.

So remember that no matter who we are, or how successful we become, that impostor syndrome is always there, ready to unleash itself. It's up to you to recognise when it's creeping up so you can start to deal with it before it ends up controlling your decisions and getting in the way of your goals.

If you are currently struggling with that inner critic and would like some more help dealing with it, please get in touch with me via the QR code below and we can have a chat.

Chapter 4: The 100k Club

Setting your income goal

You've got your business idea and now it's time to act on it. To see your idea through, you are going to need some cash to propel you forward, and an income goal that inspires you. The 100k Club is a concept based around setting income goals. Earning £100k was the first income goal I set myself. This was also the qualification to sign up for the Strategic Coach® Programme, although I had been to many taster sessions (so many that Paulette Sopoci, a presenter at many of the sessions I attended, thought I must be on the Programme).

At this time, I heard Jack Canfield speak at a conference. He talked about how he wrote a cheque (check) for $1 million and stuck it to the ceiling above his bed, so that it was the last thing he saw before he went to sleep and the first thing he saw when he woke up. Personally I prefer to see my wife before I go to sleep, but whatever works for you!

This was the time when I first started setting myself goals. The first goal I wrote down was for my business to make £100k. You might think that I could have aimed higher, because although £100k is a lot of money, in the world of business this is still quite a modest figure. So yes, I could have set a loftier goal. But when you start goal setting it's important that you don't make your goals too big, or it can feel overwhelming and unachievable. Be realistic; if you're only earning £20,000 but set your sights on earning £1 million within a couple of years, your brain goes, "Nope, not going to happen" and then (guess what?) nothing happens. The inner critic wins and impostor syndrome takes over.

You need to be a bit more modest with your expectations; what matters is that the income goal is appropriate and means something to you. And remember that when you achieve a goal, you can then set a bigger one because you've got more confidence.

Why £100k?

The £100,000 figure just made sense to me. This was also the qualification to sign up for the Strategic Coach® Programme, which I was keen to join having been to many of their taster sessions. I was already earning over £50,000 in my business, so it wasn't too much of a stretch to see it increasing to that £100k. As I got closer to that £100k figure, and then when my turnover surpassed it, everything made sense. It was time to set a new goal.

I decided to stick with the £100k figure because I was familiar with it, but this time I was aiming for £100,000 in net profit, not just turnover. With all the expenses I have, that meant turnover in my business needed to be closer to £130,000, so that the figure I put on my annual tax return could be £100,000 in net profit.

For me, having that £100k as a goal has worked for a multitude of progressions. It's one that you can concentrate on without making it too hard for the reticular cortex in your brain, which is vital for goal setting. In case you're not familiar with the reticular cortex, this is the part of your brain that filters out all the external stimuli and allows you to focus. You just have to tell it what you want. In this case, I told it I wanted £100k, first in turnover and then net profit.

Of course, you can't stick with £100k forever. Once I reached £100k in net profit, I decided it was time for a bigger goal. This time, I decided I wanted £200,000 in turnover, and so the process started again. Reaching this income goal also ticked another goal off my list, which was to qualify for Court of the Table of the Million Dollar Round Table (MDRT), putting me in the top 2%(ish) of financial advisers globally. I achieved this based on my production for the year ending 2014, remembering that just three years earlier I was on the edge of bankruptcy.

But as I was getting close to that £200,000 figure for my turnover, I decided I should increase it to £250,000. I first wrote that as a goal in late 2013. When my wife Bonnie did my accounts for the year ending March 2019, lo and behold, my turnover was a little over £250,000 (well, £250,266 to be exact). Ok, it took me a while to move from under £200,000 to just over £250,000, but sometimes I am a slow learner, and I get distracted along the way.

It was crazy to see that I was less than £1,000 over that goal figure. At this point, I decided I should change my goal again to be something more sensible. In March 2018, I had a feeling that we were getting close to the £250,000 figure, so I increased my goal to £500,000. As you saw earlier, my premonition was right: we were going to hit £250,000 and in fact had exceeded it by a very small margin. It's important to be aware of what is going on, and adjust your goals accordingly. And, as you saw in the last chapter, that one phone call helped me directly achieve my goal. Although that might seem like a lucky break, remember that it was all my previous effort that brought that call to me. Hard work pays off.

Why setting income goals is important

Setting goals of any kind is important. They help keep you on track, even when you write them down, put them in a drawer and don't look at them for several years. There's a reason why goal setting works. Your subconscious brain can't tell the difference between the truth and the subliminal message. It just takes what you're feeding it as gospel.

When it comes to your income, you need to focus. Otherwise, especially when you're doing ok, you find that you're meandering through life. When you meander, you spend too much money and that means things will never improve for you.

I was in the same situation until I started my 100k Club. I was making money in the business, I was doing ok, but then a tax bill would come along and all the money would get spent on that. Setting an income goal is smart. It makes sense to have a goal to earn a certain amount of income, because then not only can you make sure you've got enough to pay your taxes, but more importantly that you've got enough to live your life the way you really want to live it.

How to start your own 100k Club

Thinking about goals is one thing, but writing them down creates a proper connection in your brain, which is why written goals are more effective than just thoughts.

Think about the last time you left the house to go shopping. Perhaps as you were walking out of the door your partner said, "Can you get two loaves of bread and a pint of milk?" You said, "Yes." But although it went in, it didn't stick. As soon as you got to the supermarket, you found yourself wandering around the aisles thinking, "What was I supposed to buy?" This is why I always write a list in my phone, because firstly it makes a proper connection in my brain, so I'm more likely to remember it, and secondly it acts as a fail-safe in case I forget.

It's the same with your goals. Writing them down is important because it creates that connection within your brain and this means you're more likely to achieve them. That's the first step to creating your own 100k Club, writing down your income goals (and your other goals, but we'll come to those later).

Because your brain accepts what you're telling it, you need to write your goals in the present tense. For example, "I drive...", "I earn...", "I am happily married", and so on. It's about placing your focus in the right place.

Take me as an example. If you looked at my desk, which is invariably covered in dozens of Post-it notes, paperwork and goodness knows what else, you would probably wonder how I get anything done, let alone run a business which, at the time, was turning over £250,000 with just two part-time members of staff.

There are always dozens of small jobs that are vying for your attention, but which of those is going to get you closer to your goals, whether that's in terms of your income or something else you're aiming for? By writing out your goals, you're showing your brain where to focus and what distractions to cut out.

One of the reasons why I'm able to cut out a lot of those distractions is because my two part-time members of staff are great at digging into detail and following through on jobs. They're the opposite of me in that respect. I take initiative, I start things, but I'm not good at following through and completing those things. In my team, we all play to our strengths. I can come up with new ideas and get projects started, and my team is great at taking those ideas through to completion.

Because they take those distractions away from me, I'm able to focus on the areas that are important not only for my income goals, but for my other goals as well.

As I mentioned earlier in the chapter, when you're setting goals, especially around your income, you need to be realistic. Goals have to be **SMART** (I'll talk more about this in the next chapter).

When you're working in financial services, the sky is almost the limit for your income. There will be thousands and thousands of people within a three-mile radius of where you live and work who need your help. But what you have to remember is that it will take time and practice to get there. We all have to start somewhere, and I would say that a good place to start with your income goal is quite a bit above making ends meet.

Start at the beginning so that you know what that figure is. Know what it's going to take for you to be earning to make ends meet. And if that's what you have to do right now, focus on that. Keep it simple and change your goals as you and your business grow.

The point is, this isn't so much about the £100k, but about the goal to get there. You have to work out whatever that figure needs to be and join whatever club works for you.

Chapter 5: Happy Wife, Happy Life???

Why this isn't a SMART goal

We all know that our goals need to be smart, but knowing that is different to knowing what defines a smart goal. There can be slight variation in how you define a smart goal, but I believe there are five key elements to a SMART goal.

A goal needs to be:

- **S**pecific
- **M**easurable
- **A**chievable
- **R**ealistic
- **T**rackable

Then it's SMART.

The title of this chapter is "Happy Wife, Happy Life", but is that a SMART goal? I would argue it's not. Why?

Is it specific...? No, because it doesn't define happiness.

Is it measurable...? No, because it relates to someone else's emotional state.

Is it achievable...? No, because no one can be happy all the time.

Is it realistic...? No, again because no one can be happy all the time.

Is it trackable...? No, because your state of happiness fluctuates.

I'm not saying you should give up on trying to make your wife, partner or a loved one happy, far from it. But what I am saying is that, in terms of goal setting, this isn't a SMART goal. It's not something you can achieve. It is out of your control.

When you get a goal that becomes impossible and doesn't fit the SMART criteria, you have to change it. I realised this and changed my goal from "Having a happy wife" to "Having a happier wife". This goal is always a work in progress, but it's also something I can always work towards.

Is it specific...? Yes, because I know precisely the little actions I can take throughout the day to make my wife happier.

Is it measurable...? Yes, because I certainly know the days when Bonnie acts happier vs the days when she's upset.

Is it achievable...? Of course! Even if I make her smile an extra few times during the day, that's worth it to me.

Is it realistic...? Yes. Anyone can make their partner that little bit happier if they make an effort.

Is it trackable...? Yes. By making an effort every day, I can certainly see the progress we have made over the years!

My story with my wife isn't uncommon, you may have a similar one with your partner. Like a lot of people in my position, self-employed, running my own business from home, I worked with my wife Bonnie. While it's great to have a supportive partner, working together isn't always the best idea.

Bonnie and I worked together for eight years (from 2006 to 2014) before we acknowledged it wasn't a good plan. During the first two weeks that Bonnie worked for me, she cried multiple times during her training. We'd argue, I'd lose my patience. I'm the first to admit that my training style isn't the best in the world, but after those two weeks she said something that really hit home.

Bonnie said, "I know that you're considerably more patient with your clients than you are with me." And she was right, but to me that felt wrong. We should all be as calm, patient, gentle and kind with our significant others as we are with the rest of the world. But more often than not, we aren't.

For those eight years, Bonnie helped the business a lot. She got stuck in and did a lot of the admin work, but she didn't enjoy it. We reached a point where I realised she needed to do something else, so I told her that I thought she needed to find something that she wanted to do, rather than helping me because she thought she should (isn't that a really cool and kind way to sack someone!).

Bonnie's initial concern was that she'd have to find a part-time job to pay the income of the person who came in and took her admin job. But what I realised was that, if I had someone working for me, as my employee, I could tell them exactly what I wanted them to do. There wouldn't be any arguments, I would be kinder and together we'd get more work done and probably generate more business.

Having a part-time employee would allow me to concentrate on the things I needed to do, knowing that I had a support person doing the jobs that I wanted them to do. Having the opportunity to concentrate in this way did, indeed, bring in more business and that's how we made up the money we needed to pay for that person. Bonnie has continued to do the books, which she enjoys, but now she doesn't do any of the admin tasks, which she hated.

Instead, she has found a new passion and decided to follow her goal of becoming an interior designer, which she loves. Now Bonnie is constantly working on our home as her first project to gain some confidence before starting up; and being able to step away from the admin and focus on what she enjoys has made her much happier. So I've also achieved my goal of having a happier wife, and now the house looks amazing too which is a nice added bonus!!

When you're setting goals, you have to keep asking yourself if they're SMART. Are they specific? Are they measurable? Are they achievable? Are they realistic? Are they trackable? If the answer to any of those questions is "no", you have to change the goal so that you come up with five "yeses".

Think back to the last chapter and your income goal. If you say that you want to have £1 million in turnover but you only have 15 clients, that's not realistic and that makes it demotivating. Whereas, if you set your goal for £100,000 in turnover, that's specific, it's certainly measurable, and for anyone working in financial services, it's achievable and therefore realistic. You can track your progress towards it and see when you've reached it. It's a SMART goal.

These conditions don't just apply to financial goals. They apply to goals in all areas of your life. You might want to lose weight, drive a specific car (or in my case it's a motorcycle – first it was a Harley Davidson 1200 Custom Sportster and then my Harley Davidson Fatboy Special; I got the 1200 Custom in 2006/7 but had to sell it in 2012, at which point I started craving the Fatboy), have a certain amount of time off, and so on. Whatever goals you have, if you make them SMART you can achieve them.

Set goals early

I strongly advise you to start setting goals as early as you can in your business life. At the time of writing this, I'm 58 years old. At this stage of my career, do I want to be building an organisation where there are five financial advisers, 20 admin staff and a monthly advertising budget of £20,000 to generate leads? The answer is probably not.

If you're 30 or 35 and you're getting started in the industry, there's no reason why you can't build a massive organisation, but you need to understand what that entails. It's important to be clear about your long-term vision, how you plan to shape your business to that, and whether that means employing staff or outsourcing. A strong vision that creates a win-win for you and your clients helps you move forward with greater clarity, momentum and purpose.

To achieve this, you've got to set your goals early and set your processes up to enable the business to grow. You need to decide that this is the kind of business you want, rather than a lifestyle business where you, as an individual, are still dealing with people and customers.

Remember that your first goal when you're starting out should always be to make ends meet, plus your tax on top. Don't forget about the tax! If you've only got to turn over £40,000 to make ends meet, but you have to give £7,500 to the tax collector at the end of the year, then actually you need to bring in £50,000 to make ends meet.

Always remember the **SMART** acronym, and if a goal is impossible, then you change it. We want to be working towards something more specific, measurable, achievable, realistic and trackable, like having a happier wife, rather than the impossible ideal of a 100% happy wife.

Chapter 5: Happy Wife, Happy Life???

Chapter 6: Leaving the Garden Shed Behind

Setting up your environment

Most of us accept that we need to have the right kind of environment in order to be productive at work. But when you're starting out it can be difficult to create the kind of professional environment you need to launch and grow your business. Small businesses often start by working out of their own homes. While I've been there and done that, I'm going to explain why you need to make a dedicated office space a priority.

Starting out

When I started my business I was living in a smaller property than the one I have now. Many new entrepreneurs find themselves in this position, where you're either working from the bedroom, the dining-room table or the kitchen. You've got your laptop and files everywhere and things can get a bit messy. If you're living with a partner, it can be especially difficult.

In the house that Bonnie and I shared at this time, there wasn't any space for a separate office, so we bought a shed for the garden. I'm doing it a disservice by calling it a shed really, it was more like a garden room. It had electricity and an internet connection, so I worked from there for a year or so.

After about a year, my parents passed away and I received an inheritance, so we were able to move to a larger house with a fourth bedroom and a study downstairs. That made things easier, but it was still far from ideal. You can't really bring clients to your home. We also had dogs and, while I always thought they were an excellent judge of someone's character, again it's not ideal to be meeting clients in your home with your dogs racing about. That said, I do know a business owner who is making a success of working from home with alpacas wandering around! I'd love you to hear more from Claire Sweet, who is a financial adviser and money coach. You can listen to our podcast chat by scanning the QR code below. It will take you straight over to my expert content page:

Although the Covid-19 pandemic certainly accelerated people's willingness to use technology, it can be hard to run a professional business from home if you choose to have in-person client meetings.

When you want to employ someone to help you out, it also makes things difficult if you're working from home. When Bonnie and I moved, I had staff coming to our home to work for me. But it always felt a bit awkward to have my team members just wandering into the kitchen to make a coffee or tea, especially after Bonnie stopped working for me.

The other downside to working from your home is that it's difficult to switch off when you have reminders of your work right in front of you.

Finding your space

My first piece of advice, therefore, is to get yourself into a position where you're not working from home. One option is to explore serviced offices so that you can leave your garden shed or bedroom behind.

When you start looking for an office, think about both what you need it for now and what you'll need it for in the future. Plan accordingly. It's better to have a space your business can grow into, and which can accommodate staff if necessary.

You should also think carefully about how you set up your working environment. For example, we have one large office with a smaller office within it, which is my domain. It's ideal because it means I can close the door when I need some peace and quiet, and it gives me private space to meet clients. It also allows me to have some separation from my team. It's great to be available, but sometimes you need a place to work without interruptions.

For me, setting up the right environment is essential for helping you find a good work-life balance.

Working efficiently

When you have an office, it also allows you to work more efficiently and you can invite people to come to you which can save you many hours of travel. It will allow you to be much more productive in your working day and make effective use of your time.

With technology and online video conferencing tools there's no reason why you can't retain clients who are based further away and predominantly work with them using virtual systems.

These days, thanks to technology, many entrepreneurs can provide the same level of service remotely as face to face, but getting those clients through the door initially can be tricky. There are a number of things to consider when you are structuring new client meetings, including how that client came to find you, the product or service you are offering, and their proposed level of investment.

If a client has come to you as a referral, then a lot of the trust has already been established and it might be that a phone or video call is sufficient to build on that relationship and close the deal. However, if the person is entirely new to you and you are selling a product of £5k or more, for example, the chances are they will prefer a face-to-face meeting before committing.

As a general rule, you might find that phone calls are sufficient for low-level investments of, say, £200; you can likely sell £1k products via video calls; and then beyond that, certainly for an initial investment of £5k or more, in-person meetings are preferable so that you can get to know the client and build trust.

Don't let your office hold you back

If you plan to build an in-person team but work from your home office for too long, or invest in too small an office, you'll stunt your business growth. Think ahead: know the space you need for storage, for equipment or files, and know that buying into an office space now that both meets current needs and allows for modest expansion gives you choices.

If you do most of your business face to face, having a proper office also supports your professionalism and how you come across to clients. However, it's equally important to avoid falling into the trap of never feeling satisfied with your work environment. It can be easy to think that you need somewhere bigger, swankier or nicer, or that you need new equipment even though what you have is perfectly serviceable. Weigh up your practical needs versus your desires, consider if there is real benefit to your clients, and think about how it impacts on profit before making a decision on a dedicated office space.

You need to get the balance right between creating a funky environment that you're going to enjoy working in and that your clients will enjoy coming to, and one that clients are going to visit and start getting concerned about how much you might charge them. You want your office to reflect the fact that you're a high-quality organisation, but you need to get the balance right because it can be easy to get carried away.

Keeping your team happy

Your team is a vital part of your environment and you should want them to be happy when they're at work. Keeping your team happy doesn't have to cost a lot of money. Simple gestures can go a long way. I always make sure that my team has everything they're going to need for work. If they tell me they've run out of something, I'll make sure I order replacements to arrive the next day.

One of my team could be described as being a bit short, so I bought her a little step to go under her chair and make sure she is comfortable when sitting at her desk. You should never hold back on small things like this. I've always found that if you're supportive of people's needs and give them what they ask for, within reason, they don't take advantage of your good nature.

It doesn't cost you a lot of money as a business owner, but it keeps everyone happy and you can't put a price on that. It's important not to assume what will make people happy though. Ask your team what they need or want from their environment and do your best to provide it. Remember that everyone is different.

For example, I bring my team Lindt chocolate probably once every three weeks or so. It's just a small gesture but it creates an amazingly friendly atmosphere among the team. It's just a nice little perk, and I make sure I don't always bring chocolate on the same day at the same point in the month so that it's always a nice surprise, rather than something people expect. It works both ways, too. One of my team bought me a bag of Revels the other day because they know how much I love those chocolates. It's a reciprocal thing that creates a happy working environment.

You'd be amazed by what you can achieve when you have a happy and friendly environment at work.

How you influence the environment

You have to remember that your disposition has as much of an impact on your environment as anything else and this is something you can control.

Sadly, there are some people out there who don't have the right disposition – whether that's because they're not happy with their lot, they're not happy with their environment or their expectations are just too high – and they choose not to change it. You have to make sure that you are happy and friendly when you're around your team. Alternatively, you could spend your time replacing staff every couple of months. However, due to the time and the expense that goes with that, it's not a good alternative.

Likewise, you want to make sure that your environment gives you a positive feeling. For example, I find that I feel drained and lose motivation when my office is a mess. In fact, this happened not so long ago. On the Friday, my team told me not to worry and, sure enough, when I came in on Monday morning they'd tidied everything up and I instantly felt more positive.

It's important to remember that being in a cramped and messy environment will affect your mood, probably make you grumpy, and add to not only your stress but also your team's stress.

Just be nice

My golden rule is to be nice to everybody you come into contact with. The world goes round much better and you get things done so much more quickly when you're nice.

If I need help with something, I often start my conversations with the phrase, "Look, I'm in a little bit of a pickle and I really need some help." And if the other person is a reasonable human being, they'll want to help.

By contrast, if you pick up the phone and start screaming and shouting, or effing and jeffing, at the person on the other end, they'll say everything you want to hear just to get you off the phone. But I guarantee if your file is in a pile of 20 others, it won't be getting anywhere near the top soon.

I'll close this chapter with a story about why it pays to be nice.

I was in India and I lost my passport. The frustrating thing was that it fell out of my pocket on the plane and I knew exactly where it would be, only, of course, I couldn't go and retrieve it. That meant I had to go to the consulate in New Delhi to get a new passport. Luckily, the guy I was with was a police officer, so he could sign my passport photo. That meant I was able to get a new passport within 24 hours.

However, that wasn't the only thing I needed in order to continue my travels. I also needed to apply for a new exit visa. I was due to leave two days later, but I wouldn't be able to get my flight without that visa. I had to miss a trip to the Taj Mahal to stay in New Delhi and sort all of this out.

The visa office was quite busy and there was a girl there who wanted to catch a flight that night. She also needed an exit visa and she kept pleading, not very nicely, almost indignantly, with the customs officer to deal with her application next. She went on and on, telling him that he had to deal with her application, and he kept telling her that he didn't and would get to it in time.

At one point, he left his desk and I watched her reach behind and move her application higher up the pile on his desk. Of course, when he came back he noticed and he made a specific point of moving her application back down the table. All I kept thinking was, just be nice. Maybe if she had been nice, he would have dealt with her application more quickly and she could have made her flight. I managed to get on mine. Think about it: a replacement passport and an exit visa in New Delhi in less than three days. Just be nice. (I do need to go back to India as I still haven't seen the Taj Mahal.)

Chapter 7: When There's Too Much Month at the End of the Money

Budgeting and clearing debts

I'd like to start by telling you how I learned the hard way about the importance of budgeting and clearing debt.

It was 2007 and I'd just received my inheritance after my parents passed away. Bonnie and I bought our new, bigger house and moved in, in August of that year. The business was doing well. I was arranging 15 to 20 mortgages a month, as well as all of the life insurance that goes with them. We had a big mortgage on the house, but that wasn't a problem. I bought myself a decent Mercedes, which was one of my goals, a coupe, using a bit of finance. Everything was great. Until...

The global financial crisis hit. It was as though the tap had been turned off. I went from arranging 15 to 20 mortgages a month for the majority of 2007 to probably doing a maximum of 25 mortgages for the whole of 2008. Our lives suddenly became very difficult. We took in lodgers to help earn a bit of extra money. We rented out our driveway.

Many business owners will have found themselves in a tight spot during the Covid-19 pandemic. It's always wise to have a contingency plan. You might never need it, but you don't want to be in a position where you do and you have no back-up.

It became trickier and trickier to pay the mortgage and cover all of our bills. Before too long we'd racked up a six-figure debt. We were constantly juggling to try to make ends meet. By 2010, I realised we needed some help and we had to rearrange our finances to give us a more affordable monthly payment.

In spite of all of this, I still think we were lucky. We had support from our business network, which allowed us to continue working. I don't know what I'd have done if I hadn't been able to carry on in the financial services industry. But this was an incredibly difficult time. We had no spare money whatsoever. As you can imagine, Bonnie wasn't happy, but I still needed to focus on the business and couldn't afford to panic or worry. I had to take positive action.

Because we weren't able to borrow any money, we had to develop the business on a shoestring budget. I poured all of my energy into making sure that all of my clients were looked after and that we were providing as good a standard of advice as we possibly could.

I would advise that when you're under pressure financially, you take extra care about what you let your mind think about and what you get involved with. It's easy to be tempted by the promise of extra money now, but it can cost you more in the long term than you gain in the short term. Stay true to yourself and your business goals, and put your clients' best interests at the heart of all that you do.

Budgeting from the start

One of the best pieces of advice I can give you is to think very carefully about your budget when you start your business. Know how much you need to earn to make ends meet. You need to know your living expenses, as well as what the bills are to run your business. This includes everything, from the cost of your office to things like advertising and marketing, because you will need a budget to get the word out there, whether you're using social media or more traditional means. The most important thing is to make sure that you have a budget for all of these expenses.

You also have to make sure that you're sensible about how you spend your money once you start earning. You might have a solid month of income, way more than you need, but don't rush to spend all the money you're making above your outgoings. My advice would be to put this extra money in reserve.

Let's take a look at an example budget to see how much money you'll need to be making to cover all of your expenses.

Imagine that all of your personal bills – that's the mortgage, energy, broadband, phone, food and so on – come in at £3,000 a month. Then you need to allow another £1,000 a month for running the business, covering your fees for transacting and so on. On top of that, you need to allow money for tax, because the tax collector will want to take their slice regularly too.

Tax is something that a lot of people forget about. If you've earned £3,000 a month, that's £36,000 in annual profit, which means, to all intents and purposes, you've got another £8,000–£10,000 in tax to allow for. It's not something you want to forget in your calculations or you're in for a nasty surprise! I had far too many of those in my early years...

You also need to know how much you are going to charge for your services. I have had a number of conversations and seen examples where the session/service rate charged to make ends meet meant that the number of clients needed was more than one could realistically see in a week/month.

Say you need to earn £3,000 a month and you charge £50

per session – this means you need to do 60 sessions per month, which is only 15 per week, or three per day. That doesn't sound a lot, but when you do some market research you find that a busy established business is doing five per day, and sometimes less. You are starting from scratch and you need to dive in at 60% capacity of an established business from day one. You are also travelling to see your clients, so now you need a decent car and you need to cover the cost of fuel. Before you know it, to earn £3,000 you have to do more business each month than the established business. Pay very careful attention to your figures and your targets, make them SMART.

The difference between being a salesperson and running a business

What you have to remember when you set up your own business is that it's not the same as being a salesperson. Of course, you need to sell, but there's so much more to it than that. This is a mistake that a lot of people who've spent their lives working at firms make.

When you're working for a firm, you might be an amazing salesperson, taking £10,000 of sales a month. However, you have to appreciate all the support you're getting there that allows you to make those sales, and that support doesn't cost you a penny while you're an employee. I'm talking about admin support, people answering the phones, marketing support and so on.

When you go out on your own, you've got to do all of that yourself. All of a sudden, you can't spend your whole day selling because you have to make time to do all the admin, the accounts, the marketing, answer the phones. You'll find that 60–70% of your time isn't spent on sales any more; it's spent on all those other tasks that you took for granted as being done by other people when you worked for a firm.

This then means that when you do meet with clients, you're

under pressure to sell. Trust me when I tell you that when you're under pressure to make a sale, a client knows it. You can be the best actor in the world, but I guarantee they'll be able to tell when you're desperate to make a sale.

My advice when you're starting out is to set your expectations at a reasonable level. Make sure that you account for everything, both in terms of your budget and what you'll need to spend your time doing.

How to market your business on a shoestring

As I mentioned earlier, following the financial crash, we were forced to run our business on a shoestring. We didn't have the money to send our clients swanky brochures, but there are lots of small and cheap – if not free – things you can do to market your business.

We focused on keeping in touch with our existing clients on a regular basis in the most affordable way possible: email. I wanted to make sure that they had everything they could possibly need and that they got the best service possible, because that meant I was more likely to get referrals. These are a big factor in being successful in your business.

Even if you're operating on a budget, don't use that as an excuse to not have certain things. In the last chapter, I talked about leaving the garden shed behind and setting up the right environment. This is absolutely worth doing even when you don't have a lot of spare money available.

If you look around, you can find affordable serviced offices where you can operate from. How affordable is going to depend on where you're based, but there are opportunities in most places; and by setting up in an office space rather than continuing to work from your shed, you'll find new clients and make new, often bigger, deals.

Before I moved out of my house into a serviced office, I used to go to the gym quite regularly, and on my way there, I'd pass a building that had a sign up for serviced offices. One day, Bonnie mentioned how nice it was on a Friday because I'd always be out and about that day, and my staff didn't work on Fridays. She said it was great to have the house to herself, and that was the not-so-subliminal trigger for me to look for a dedicated office space.

Of course, I thought of the building I passed every day, so I took a space in this serviced office. For a start, it was great at helping me stick to a working regime. But there was another benefit that I hadn't initially considered – I started meeting new people.

When you start working in a block of serviced offices, you'll be in there with all kinds of other people; you're quite likely to be the only business of your type, so there's always a possibility that you'll pick up new business. Going back to the point I made in the last chapter about the importance of being nice, this applies when you're sharing a building with other businesses too.

A smile and a hello as you're walking down the corridor can go a long way. One of the simple things that we did was to put a branded notepad in everyone's pigeonhole at Christmas. It was our way of saying Merry Christmas and just letting everyone know that we were there. I also gave some to the maintenance office.

The nice thing is that a short while later, one of the guys on the maintenance team came up to me to thank me for the notepad and tell me that it had been really useful. It also meant I got first options on a bigger office when it became available.

Now, this little gesture didn't cost us more than about £200 for around 150 notepads. It didn't take a lot of effort on our part either, but it did get us noticed and help me to start building relationships with the other people in the office building.

Don't forget about your personal life

I'll close this chapter by summarising the most important things to remember when it comes to budgeting and taking care of your money.

One of the key things is keeping an eye on your numbers and making sure that you don't forget people like the tax collector when you're calculating your budget. Make sure you know how much it will cost you to exist each month. Once you know that, you can work out what you need to do month by month, business-wise, to satisfy that need.

However, while you're looking at your business costs and how much you need to make, don't take your eyes off your personal life. For example, if you have a young family and a stay-at-home partner, you might have a goal that you don't want them to have to work while the children grow up. If that's the case, you need to account for this when you're calculating your budget.

I can tell you from experience that it's incredibly stressful for your relationship when you have too much month at the end of the money. When Bonnie and I were in this position and working together it caused a lot of stress. And stress is a killer. It doesn't only kill you in the literal sense, but it also kills your appetite for life and your "get up and go". You need to make time to talk about money and budget as a couple.

Whenever I sit down with a couple, I tell them to set up a joint account for their bills but to make sure they each keep their own personal account so that they can do nice things for themselves and their partner without them necessarily knowing how much it costs. When I'm talking to a couple about this, I usually tell them to buy each other little things, like a bunch of flowers every now and then, and see how their world lights up. Normally one of them will chuckle and say that they've never bought flowers or little gifts, so it's a nice thing to do just because; not because it's their birthday or your anniversary. Those small gestures make a difference.

The other thing to remember about having a joint account for bills is to make sure you transfer the amount for your share of the bills into it the day after payday (you've then paid all your bills on one day). However, once your money has gone in there each month, you can't think of it as your money any more. That money is spoken for and you shouldn't dip into it for any other reason. You have to protect it.

There are two other things that I advise people to save for by putting money aside each month: holidays (vacations) and Christmas. I'm always amazed by how many people seem to be surprised by Christmas. It always falls on 25 December and you know that it's going to come around every year, because it has for over 2000 years. Yet, every year, people get caught out. They put "Christmas" on their credit card and then they have to find a way to pay it off afterwards. Whereas, if they just put £75 a month aside for 12 months, they'd have £900 to spend on Christmas, without having to go near a credit card.

My other piece of advice for you when it comes to the likes of Christmas is to spend your money on experiences that you can share with your loved ones rather than on material items. After all, there's only so much space in a house. The average garage doesn't have a car in it, but is instead somewhere that people store all manner of things they never or rarely use. Don't contribute to that problem, and try not to give in to the pressure to buy new material possessions you don't need.

The same principle applies with saving for holidays. Too many people put their holidays on their credit cards and then have the stress of paying them off afterwards, which often negates the good that a holiday does. If you put £100 a month into your holiday fund, it means you can have a pot of money to spend on whatever kind of trip you want. The key is treating it like another bill and saving for it accordingly.

If you budget correctly and allow for all the costs of both your business and personal life, you will hopefully avoid running into the scenario of having too much month at the end of the money. If you would like to access some simple tools to get you started in this arena, get in touch! You can email me at doug@dougbennett.co.uk.

Sarah's Story

How does that sound?

In April 2018 I met Doug and this couldn't have come at a better time for me. I'm a mortgage and financial adviser in New Zealand, covering mortgages and risk insurance. I started my business in October 2015, adding risk insurance in 2017. I'm a single parent with teenagers, and still relatively new to financial services. By the time I met Doug, my business had stopped. In February/March 2018, it was almost as though someone had just decided I wasn't going to have any more business.

However, although my business had slowed right down, I was still travelling to the Gold Coast in Australia for the first overseas conference being hosted by my network. I'd paid for the trip, so I decided I may as well go. Before I go to any conference, I always like to see who the speakers will be and I'd noticed Doug in the line-up before I travelled. I even connected with him on LinkedIn before the conference and told him I was looking forward to hearing him talk. Of course, he replied and said he looked forward to seeing me there.

When Doug stood up on stage he told his amazing story. I'm a big believer in the idea that you can't get to the very top without being at the bottom, experiencing some ups and downs along the way and climbing back to the top. I don't believe you can go from the bottom to the top without some kind of dip in the middle. After Doug had told his story, I decided that I'd go over and introduce myself.

As well as meeting Doug, I also met his wife Bonnie and we even all went for coffee together. As if to demonstrate how small the world is, we even realised that Crawley, where Doug and Bonnie live, was where I'd lived with my now ex-husband many years ago. In fact, my father-in-law lived just 1.6 miles from Doug's office. That was the beginning of my friendship with Doug. When I look back I feel as though I was meant to meet him. I could have very easily not gone to the conference, because money was so tight in my business, and I could have just as easily not introduced myself to him after his talk.

But I went and I made the effort to meet him in person and those decisions have changed my life.

As I said, my business had stalled. At this point, I was making very little money. However, I still had a mortgage to pay and, of course, I was supporting my children. I didn't have money coming in from elsewhere so I knew I needed to be successful with this. I couldn't take any more credit cards out and the ones I had were full. I actually had to borrow some money from friends and I was considering selling my car, just to get the $8,000–$10,000 out of that.

When I returned to New Zealand after that conference I was really struggling. I'm not someone who finds it easy to ask for help. In fact, I don't even like the phrase "reaching out for help", but I stayed in touch with Doug and at some point I felt bold enough to ask him to help me. He was really lovely and told me that he'd be happy to chat to me every now and then.

This was around May/June 2018. Because there's always an 11, 12 or 13-hour time difference between the UK and New Zealand, Doug used to call me in the mornings when he was out walking his dogs, which meant it was evening for me. It was just perfect. Doug and I used to check in once a week and we'd talk about my business. I used to tell him about specific clients and ask his advice. As soon as we started talking regularly, it was as though I had this little person on my shoulder called Doug talking to me all the time.

Reaching out was a really big thing for me to do, and I think at the stage that Doug and I started talking regularly, I was at the bottom of my heap. But what you realise is that if you're at the bottom of your heap, you're not going to see wealth come to you. It's about your mentality and focus, and making sure that you open up to the world so that good things can come to you.

Doug encouraged me to really think about how I was looking after my clients, how I was talking to them, what I'd do if they tried to reduce the amount of insurance they took out to a level below what they needed and so on. And this worked both ways: I knew that he was helping me a lot but I also helped him with some ideas for his business.

That was also a big confidence booster for me, to be able to give Doug some ideas and different words and phrases to use too. But that's the thing about connections like this – we're both different people with different personalities who use different words to speak to clients, and sometimes it can really help to have a different perspective.

Aiming for MDRT

Doug was determined to help me get to Million Dollar Round Table (MDRT). At this point, I hadn't been doing insurance for that long, but in your first year you can apply for MDRT as what's called an Aspirant, where you have to get 50% of the normal qualification you need. I remember that it went right to the wire that Christmas.

Doug was always encouraging me. He would ask me how

much more I needed to get and then he'd make me work out how many months and weeks we had to go, and how many policies I'd need to sell in New Zealand to hit that figure. He got me to divide this down into weeks, rather than months, which made it feel more manageable. I'd always be thinking about which client was warm, which clients I could go back to. I qualified as an MDRT Aspirant that year and it was really exciting. There's a big MDRT annual conference and the MDRT members get their spaces first. Then there's a specific date in March when they open up spots to Aspirants.

Because of the time difference, I needed to be online at 2am in New Zealand to log in and register for my place at the conference. That didn't go entirely smoothly but I eventually registered and then I was really excited that I'd get to see Doug again.

In June 2019, the MDRT conference was held in Miami. To get there, I had a 15-hour flight to Houston, then a stop before I could fly to Miami. On the morning that I was due to leave New Zealand, I didn't feel too good. After an hour and a half I realised it could be something serious, so I phoned an ambulance for myself. I was rushed to hospital where they discovered I had kidney stones. It was really painful and I was dosed up on morphine. I don't remember a great deal, except that every time I saw a doctor I'd ask if there was any chance I could fly the following day, because that would have enabled me to make it for the conference.

I remember one doctor leaning over me and saying, "Sarah, you've had that much morphine that you're not going to be flying anywhere." And so I had to miss the conference. The feelings that overwhelmed me can't be described. I was devastated at this moment.

However, Doug didn't let me give up and he kept pushing me with goals throughout the year – he made sure it was always about the client. It went to the wire: 17 December 2019. I did my numbers and I'd qualified for MDRT as a full member! For some people, this might not seem like such a big thing, but I've only been working in insurance for just over two years and to make the numbers you need to qualify for MDRT is pretty amazing.

Why it's good to talk

One of the things I've realised is that when I talk to Doug he doesn't focus on my numbers, he focuses on my clients. It's interesting because that perspective is what makes all the difference and it's what Doug and I both have in common.

No matter what we do, we want the client to get whatever's in their best interest. That means we're not only asking the client about their finances – their numbers – but we want to know about them as people and their experiences. That means the advice you can give them is framed in a different way.

The pause

I talk very quickly, and it's one of the things that Doug has helped me to moderate. He'll often say something and then pause. He's been trying to teach me to pause more because this makes the client really think about what you're saying. It's one of the most important things I've learned from him.

Seeing my business grow

I started my business from home in 2015 and within a year I'd moved into an external office, which happened to be very smelly due to nearby restaurants. The lease came up and I moved into a tiny space, 6m x 2m in size, and it was relatively cheap to rent. But it wasn't a great space as it was so small and not ideal for bringing clients into. Ever since I started my business, I've been very clear that I need my clients to come to me – either to my office or to have virtual meetings via Zoom. I decided this was my business model. However, as I said, this space was just too small. I also realised that I needed an assistant but I didn't have space for one.

In June 2019, the business that was leasing the rest of the floor that my tiny office was on moved out. I saw an opportunity so I leased the whole floor. By August, I was able to hire my first full-time employee, Helena. I gave her the title Client Manager. I didn't want to just call her my assistant, because she's so much more than that. I made a very conscious decision to take someone on full time and to pay them a good salary, because I wanted a good person.

When I look back now at where I was just one year earlier, April 2018, at rock bottom and reaching out for help from Doug, I'm amazed. My initial goal was to build my income back up and put myself back out there. I hadn't considered that in just 12 months I'd have acquired a much bigger office and my first full-time employee.

I spoke to Doug a lot before I hired anyone into my business. We discussed the type of person I needed and the type of personality. It's been a big learning curve for me because I'd always been a manager of people and now I'm a doer. But after four years in business, I suddenly had to learn to let someone else do the work. Luckily I don't have to micromanage Helena at all, but then that's why I hired her. One of the things you always hear is that you should hire an assistant when you're not quite ready for one, otherwise if you wait, you'll be too busy and won't have the time to train them properly. So it was a leap of faith for me but one that has really paid off.

Riding the ups and downs

I started my business in October 2015. I've been on a crazy journey in that time and I can honestly say I don't think I'd be where I am now if it weren't for Doug and his advice and support.

When I started my business, it just seemed to be on an upward trajectory. The business was never quiet and it was all going well. But when it started to slow down I was really scared. I have a nice house, which I'd just finished renovating, and I was seriously worried I was going to lose everything. I didn't have anyone to turn to who could support me and my children financially, and asking Doug for help with my business was really hard.

What this period made me realise is that it's not enough to be outgoing and engaging, because you really need to know your stuff when you hit hard times. After speaking to Doug, I got the business rolling again and this period was actually really cool. I was able to pay back the friends I'd borrowed money from and clear my credit cards to get rid of that debt. Then it was as though I could breathe again, thank goodness.

After sorting out all my personal financial things, it was great to be able to focus on growing the business. It's been wonderful to see the transformation, especially in my office. It's really nice to be able to see where I started out, in my tiny 6m x 2m office, and compare it to where I am now: a 92sqm office that I've even renovated so that it's an enjoyable space to be in. I know without a shadow of a doubt that I couldn't have got my business back on track and achieved all of this without Doug's support.

He could tell that I was excited, that I knew my stuff and that I wanted to learn, and that's why we got on. I'm really proud of what I've achieved and that I'm able to show that women of any age can succeed in this industry. In 2019, I won three really big awards too. All of that has helped improve my credibility with clients, who can walk into my office and see those awards displayed on the wall.

Connecting, communicating and confidence

One of the reasons why I think I really hit it off with Doug, and why we've become such good friends, is that he understands how I do business. I'm not the type of person who's comfortable cold calling people. Most of my clients come from contacts, referrals and connecting with people. My business leads by mortgages first and looking after the client as a whole, and then risk insurance fits perfectly.

I also find clients through my work as a marriage celebrant. I've been working as a celebrant since 2009, and it feeds in perfectly with my work as a financial adviser. Couples remember me and then when they need help arranging a mortgage to buy their first home, or sorting out life insurance, they come to me.

I build strong connections with them because I remember little details about their wedding day. For example, there's one couple whom I married and whom I've helped a few times with organising financial products. On their wedding day, the weather wasn't great so we had to move the ceremony indoors. I was standing outside with Mary, the bride, ready to walk in for the ceremony and she turned to me and said, "Sarah, I've forgotten my veil." I looked at her and just said, "You look fabulous. He's in there. He wants to marry you. He won't care about the veil." And she walked straight in, and it was the most wonderful wedding. I find remembering small details like that about my clients' lives helps me to build those lasting connections, which then leads to them working with me in this business (along with me parking my branded car in the car park of the wedding venue!).

Communication is key to this. You need to talk and you need to listen. Doug and I communicate a lot. We talk. Sometimes I'll send him an email. It's the same with clients. You need to have regular catch-ups with them, whether that's face to face, via Zoom or just through a quick email.

It's not just about making connections with your clients either. It's about making professional connections. There are other advisers who can help you learn and grow your business, just like Doug has helped me to grow my business. It's an important mindset shift to go from seeing everyone as a competitor to realising that we're all different and that, therefore, we'll appeal to different kinds of clients.

The other thing I've learned from Doug is to have confidence in myself. You have to have the confidence to tell people your story, to explain how you fell down but then climbed back up again.

How does that sound?

This phrase, "How does that sound?" is one of the most important things that Doug has taught me. Here's how it works.

I recently had an online meeting with a couple whose wedding I performed in 2019. I've already done their insurance and at the moment I'm organising a mortgage for them. Sally and Bob are a lovely couple, you can just see that they're very connected. At the start of the meeting I just asked them what was going on in their world, how their jobs are and so on. Bob told me that he'd recently had a pay rise, so I just said, "That's great, if you email me after this call I'll see if you need to get any more insurance. How does that sound?"

We carried on chatting and ran through the other things we needed to talk about. I always like to finish any client meeting by simply summarising what we've discussed. So, in this instance, I said, "We'll just refresh what the next steps are. The next steps are that you're going to email me about your pay increase and I'm going to then check about an increase in your income protection. I'll also email you about the mortgage and we'll get that sorted in the next couple of weeks. We'll just keep the connection going. How does that sound?"

That phrase, "How does that sound?", is useful for the client and for me. Firstly, it makes me stop talking because I'm asking a question. I have to pause. It's also a question that the client can't just say "yes" or "no" to. That makes them think about their answer.

It's about communicating and keeping those lines of communication open between you and your clients.

What you can learn from me

"How does that sound?" is one of my top takeaways from Doug, but there are a number of other things that you can learn from my story.

I would certainly say that I should have asked for help earlier, although I'm glad that I reached out when I did. Don't be afraid to reach out, because you could end up with a wonderful friend like I did.

I'd also urge you not to dismiss the element of chance. Life is all about chance meetings. There were many times when Doug and I could have missed making that connection. I might not have sent him a message and connected with him on LinkedIn before the conference. I could have gone to see a different speaker that day. Or I could have chosen not to say anything to him after his talk, even though I'd been moved by it. The lesson is don't let those opportunities to meet people and connect pass you by.

You also have to remember that times change. You can't rest on your laurels. You always need to be looking for different things that you can do in business and how you can change if your business starts to stagnate. If you're a business that stays static and doesn't move with the times, you're going to get left behind.

Sometimes that might mean you have to drag your clients along with you. I've been using Zoom for meetings for a while, but with the Covid-19 pandemic, that technology has suddenly become essential. If you've got a client who is a bit of a technophobe, look at how you can make the transition easier for them. How can you make it as easy as possible for them to access and engage with the technology you're using?

You also need to make sure you're always learning. That might be by doing training, but also just by talking to other advisers. Look at how much I've learned from Doug in the time I've known him.

The difference is Doug: a lifetime of business learnings in two years

If I was to sum up my friendship with Doug so far, I'd describe it as a lifetime of business learnings in two years.

I've been in the deepest, darkest financial place of my life, and come out the other side. I could have been forced to sell my house, even though that was the last thing I wanted to do. I could have lost my business. When I met Doug, I was at a very low point. With his help, I've been able to climb back up again. This was so lucky for me, my family and my business. I'm in such a great space now.

These things are meant to test us, but I honestly don't think I'd have come so far if I hadn't had a friend like Doug sitting on my shoulder, giving me guidance when I needed it. He's a priceless friend with so much knowledge to share and, more than that, he's happy to share it with anyone who asks.

How does that sound?

Sarah Bloxham
Financial adviser
Let's Talk! Mortgages & Insurance
Auckland, New Zealand

So that's Sarah's story. If you were sharing your own business success story in six months' time, what would you say? What goals would you have accomplished? What would be your next step? If you'd like coaching and mentoring expertise to reach the next level, feel free to head over to my website using the QR code found on the following page.

Chapter 8: It's a Given

Turning up on time

Trust is like a china plate: if it's broken, you can fix it, but the cracks will always show. That was a saying I first heard at my first MDRT meeting back in 1995 and it's always stuck with me. It encapsulates exactly why you need to be trustworthy and why you need to care about your clients. But more than that, they need to know that you care about them and they need to know that what you're doing for them is ahead of your own personal interests.

Gaining trust is simple and I'd say that turning up on time is a good starting point. It's one of the fundamentals from Dan Sullivan of Strategic Coach® too: say "please" and "thank you", turn up on time and always do what you've promised to do.

The only time I didn't turn up...

I can honestly say that there's only ever been one time in my career when I didn't turn up to meet a client. I received a phone call at about 10:10am on a Monday morning from Bev, the lady I should have been meeting, asking if I was coming.

I'm based in Redhill and when I got her phone call I wasn't remotely ready to leave the house. Not to mention that she lived in Berkhamsted, which is a 45-minute journey at the best of times. It was my mistake. I'd written our meeting in my day book, but I hadn't put it in my diary.

Now, I explained and managed to arrange another meeting with her, which was good, and she's given me plenty of business over the years. The point of this story is that you can make mistakes, and we all do, but you have to make sure that you do a little bit extra to overcome them.

The importance of being early

Aside from this meeting, I've always turned up and I'm always early. Turning up on time might be the subtitle of this chapter, but really it should be "turning up early". I would say that you should aim to be at least ten minutes early for every meeting you're going to.

At one stage, I found myself in the situation where I was arriving for all of my in-person meetings about half an hour early, because my assistant was significantly overestimating how long it would take me to get anywhere. I was getting reminders to leave for meetings earlier than I needed to, and I'd just go. I often found myself arriving somewhere at least 15 minutes early, sitting there twiddling my thumbs.

However, what I realised was that those 15 minutes could be invaluable. During that time, I could visualise how the meeting would play out. I could consider the responses I might get from my client and any possible objections. It gave me time to think about how I could handle those and get the right outcome from the meeting. It meant I was calm and relaxed by the time I went in.

Contrast that to how you'd feel if you suddenly found out you had to leave the office for a meeting in 45 minutes and that it's a 45-minute drive away. You're rushing out of the door, grabbing files and paperwork as you go. Just as you get to the car, you realise you've left one of the files you needed in the office, so you run back in, get it and run back to the car.

Once you're in the car, you've got to put the address you're going to into your sat nav. While you're doing this, time is ticking away and it takes three, four, five, six minutes before you're on your way. Now, all of a sudden, you're behind schedule for that 45-minute journey. You're shouting and screaming at all the other road users who, while they're driving perfectly normally, are holding you up. You get angry. You curse every red traffic light. Then you have to ring the client to tell them you're running ten minutes late.

What kind of mindset will you be in when you arrive for that meeting? You'll be flustered, your heart rate will be elevated, you won't be thinking clearly and you're much more likely to rush through what you have to say.

By turning up ahead of time, you're setting yourself up to be in control. You'll find that the deals you do are much bigger and that everything goes much more smoothly if you're even five minutes early for a meeting. In that time, your heart rate can slow down, you can let your blood pressure drop and you'll feel more confident in the situation.

It's all about going into your meetings in the right mindset. You'll find that adding extra time to your schedule to allow you to turn up early will pay you back in dividends. You'll close bigger sales and create lasting relationships with clients.

This is equally important for online meetings and online conferences. Your clients need to see that you are prepared and that you respect and care about them. There's no excuse for turning up late, not having the right documents to hand or keeping them waiting. Your client must be your sole focus during any meeting, virtual or otherwise. Sharing a screen with a million icons on the desktop is like showing them the mess in your under-stairs cupboard.

Create a spacious, clean virtual environment, one where the client feels safe and comfortable. Think about the whole customer experience, which if virtual, includes your office backdrop, your visual and audio quality. A well-considered environment will help you both to focus and continue to build and maintain the "know, like and trust" factor.

Showing respect

Turning up early for meetings doesn't just allow you to feel more composed, it shows that you respect your client's time. If they've had to wait ten minutes for you, that doesn't reflect well, especially if they're a busy person who doesn't have ten minutes to waste in their day. It puts you on the back foot and it comes back to breaking two of those fundamental rules from Dan Sullivan of Strategic Coach®: not only are you late, but you're not doing what you promised. You promised to turn up for a meeting at a specific time and you haven't done that. It breaks trust.

The same rule of turning up early also applies to any online meetings, especially those you're hosting. You don't want to be the last person joining a meeting when you're the host.

There's a flip side to this as well. Turning up early shows that you're respecting yourself. You're giving yourself permission and time to get into a relaxed state of mind. Rushing around all the time is also one of the quickest routes to a heart attack. You need to slow things down and stay in control. Respect your time and attitude as much as you respect your client's time.

Always be prepared

When you're rushing, you miss things and you forget things. If you race into a meeting late, you're not going to be calm and composed. You're probably not going to be logical and you'll almost certainly forget something important. As soon as something unexpected pops up, you'll lose all of your momentum. By the same token, you shouldn't turn up to meetings on time or early and try to run through everything off the cuff.

You need to be prepared. Create an agenda for every meeting you're going to, even if you decide not to share it with your client in advance – and there can be good reasons for not sharing agendas. But make sure you have one nonetheless.

As a financial adviser, I make sure I get my clients to fill in relevant paperwork well in advance of us having a meeting. I'll send them the risk questionnaire in advance. I'll get them to complete a medical form before I go to see them if we're looking at anything like life insurance or critical illness cover. If I'm going to see a client about arranging a mortgage, I make sure they send me copies of their payslips and bank statements before our meeting. How best can your clients prepare before meetings to help make the most of your time together?

There are several reasons why this is a good idea. Firstly, I want to make sure I have a full picture of my client, or as full as I can at this stage. I want to go to the meeting prepared with any paperwork I might need them to sign. You're shooting yourself in the foot if you go to a meeting without that critical piece of paper or information that you need to progress.

Secondly, if you get someone to complete any necessary paperwork when you aren't there to lead or influence their answers, you'll get more honest answers from your client that will give you a truer picture of who they are.

Thirdly, if you have information in advance, you will be able to ask smarter questions and potentially save yourself time by not offering a product or service that clearly isn't useful. Often you stumble on a piece of information by chance that enables you to deepen your rapport and offer them something far more suited to their needs.

By preparing for meetings in this way, you are ensuring that your client sessions are as productive as possible and that you spend time on what's appropriate. It's about making the best use of both your time and the client's time.

Learn to delegate

Accept that you need help to do your job properly and to the best of your ability. Delegating is essential, and delegating to the right person is just as important.

Ideally what you want to do is delegate all the tasks that you're weakest at to someone else. A person who not only enjoys doing all the jobs you hate but is good at them too, should be your first hire. When you're planning to hire an assistant, start by making a list of all the business tasks that you hate. They're probably also going to be the ones you're no good at. This list should form the basis of a job description.

Don't put off getting support for too long either. Get the support you need in order to work at your greatest capability, because that will lead you to success.

I personally think that no matter what you spend on staff, you tend to get six or seven times their salary back from them in increased productivity. However, even if it is only twice as much but you have more free time, that's still a win in my book, so why wouldn't you want to get support as soon as possible?

Trying to do everything on your own also leads to situations where you turn up late for meetings. Picture the scene: you're just getting ready to leave the office when a phone call comes in, or an urgent email pops up in your inbox. Even if you don't answer the email or you take a quick phone message, this will pull your focus away from your meeting. You don't want to be running around like a mad thing all the time.

Hire an administrator (or virtual assistant) and make sure that one of their jobs is to look at your emails. In an ideal world, hardly any of the emails that come to your business should make it to your inbox.

Creative communication

In my line of work, sometimes you have to tell people things that they might not want to hear. If you have a client who's significantly overweight, for instance, you might not be able to get them critical illness cover. Or their life insurance premiums might be really high. Having time before meetings can help you think of creative ways to break what could be perceived as bad news.

However you decide to communicate bad news to people, you have to do it with a smile and show your client that it's coming from a place of honest concern. You can't escape the fact that someone who's obese and in poor health will have to pay more for life insurance than someone who's in good shape and really fit. You can explain that changing some of their lifestyle habits could improve their health, and therefore lower their life insurance premium. But you have to do this in a sensitive way, and always from a place of concern.

If your client knows that you mean well, they'll take that kind of news much better. For example, if you're a health coach or a personal trainer and a client is not getting the anticipated results, there may be times when you need to confront or challenge them about ongoing habits or behaviours for their own benefit. How might this relate to you and your business? What sort of sensitive information do you handle and how might you communicate it more creatively?

Chapter 8: It's a Given

Chapter 9: There Should Always Be Time for Beer

Plan your spare time

It can be easy to have big, hairy, audacious goals and that's great, but what you have to ask yourself is, if achieving these big, hairy, audacious goals is to the detriment of your personal life, then what's the point?

When you're putting all of your focus on building a business and working hard, your personal relationships will suffer. They deteriorate over time. You see it all the time with business people who are on their second, third or even fourth marriage.

It doesn't wash when you go home to your spouse after barely seeing them and say, "But I did it all for you." Your family deserves the same level of courtesy that you extend to your staff and clients. Do what you said you would, be on time, show them how much you care and appreciate them.

If you're completely honest with yourself, you didn't do all of these things for your partner, you did them for yourself. You're the only person who gets recognition for achieving your goals. You're the only person who sees the business growing and sees the money coming in. You're the one whose name goes on any awards you win. Ultimately, all that you achieve comes back to you; and whilst your family might benefit from luxury holidays and a higher standard of living, I'd hope they also want to experience it all with you.

When you fail to make time for your family and personal relationships, you will suddenly realise one day that your marriage is over (if it wasn't already), that your kids have grown up and you barely had any input into their development, and that you're suddenly in a lonely place.

I learned this lesson the hard way. My first marriage ended when my children were aged five and three. I was working hard all the time and I wasn't making time for them or my ex-wife. My ex-wife was working hard at the local pub. In fact, she met her future husband in that pub. So, the lesson here is that there should always be time for beer, preferably with your wife or other half. I'm not telling you this story with any bitterness attached to it. But it is important to recognise the impact that failing to make quality time for your family has on your relationships.

Whatever it is you do, remember that communication is key. For example, I usually take Fridays off to spend with Bonnie, but right now I am taking this Friday off to run a training day because I am a trustee for Us in a Bus (a charity that helps isolated people with profound learning and communication issues to find the right support and means to express themselves). My commitment to this means that my wife and I lose our day together, but I know when I explain she'll be ok with it. You just need to be clear with your communication.

Having this clear line of communication means you can be completely focused on what you are doing at the time: 100% on work when you're at work, and 100% focused on your personal life and relationships outside of that.

Finding space for quality time

We all live increasingly busy lives and it can sometimes feel like a challenge to make quality time for your loved ones. You feel as though your schedule is already full.

There's a famous story that perfectly illustrates this point and it's probably one that you've heard before.

A philosophy professor stood in front of his students with an empty jar and a bottle of beer, and proceeded to fill the jar with rocks. "Is the jar full?" he asked them when he finished, to which they replied, "Yes." Next, he took small pebbles and put them in the jar, giving it a small shake to allow them to slip between the larger rocks. Once again, he asked the question, "Is the jar full?" Once again, the students in his class said, "Yes." Finally, he took sand and poured it into the jar. Of course, the grains of sand found their way between the rocks and pebbles. When he'd finished, he asked the question again, "Is the jar full?" and again his students said, "Yes."

He then explained that the jar represents your life, and the items he'd placed in it represent the different things that you spend your time and energy on: the rocks represent the important things that have real value, such as your family, your partner, your health, your children; the pebbles represent the other things that matter, such as your job, house, car, clothes and so forth; and the sand represents everything else, all the small stuff.

If you fill your time up with small stuff, the sand, you will not be able to fit the rocks and pebbles into your life.

One of the students asked about the beer. The professor opened the beer, smiled and poured it into the jar, stating that it didn't matter how full your life was, there was always room for a beer.

The point is that you should find a balance between working

and spending time with the people you love, whoever they may be.

You might have to spend some time working hard now, and when you're scraping by it can be virtually impossible to treat yourself and your family to nice things that you otherwise might enjoy, like a nice bottle of wine or a meal out, but you have to make sure you make provision for rewards in the future.

There needs to be a demonstrable benefit to you having to work four weekends in a row, for example. So, if you have to work four weekends in a row, tell your partner that you'll go away for a weekend as soon as those four weeks are up. You also have to make sure you follow through and don't make promises you can't keep.

Ask your significant other or a close friend

If you aren't sure about your work-life balance, ask your significant other or a close friend. He or she will be able to give you a couple of clues that will leave you in no doubt.

Although it might not feel like it, there is enough time for work and for your personal life. You just need to plan both. Look at your business goal and be really, really focused on achieving it. There's an outside chance, if you're focused and you set your day up properly, that you could achieve that goal in half the time. When you do that, you have more time to prioritise other things. However, very often we spend all our time running around, trying to do this, trying to do that, trying to hit the target, and it uses up all the time available because it can.

When you have personal goals, when you know how you want to spend your personal time and with whom, you're more likely to do all you can to protect or increase that personal time. If your plan for the evening is to mess about with your phone, then there's not much incentive to finish early or on time, and that has an impact on everyone.

Communication keeps everything flowing well. I've got a Harley Davidson and what's the point in having it just sitting there if I never ride it? When it came to the four-day bank holiday weekend, there was a ride out that I wanted to go on. So because I knew I wanted to be out on the bike on Sunday morning, Bonnie and I did quite a few jobs on the Friday and Saturday so that I could go out on the Sunday and enjoy my day without any guilt or concern. We both knew what the plan was and that was good time management.

It's not about asking permission, it's about being respectful and letting your loved ones know that they matter to you. Also, by you doing what you want to do, you are happier and more present when you all have time together.

Reap the rewards

In addition to that, if you spend 100% of your time in your business, it makes you pretty dull. There's no other interesting stuff to share with anybody. People don't want to talk about your business all the time, so you need to have a life outside of it. What's more, you deserve to have a life. If you decided to be an entrepreneur to do things your way, earn more and create freedom, then why would you simply work all the time? And, from a business perspective, you need downtime to be able to work more effectively, otherwise everything will take twice as long and then you're stuck.

There has to be some reward, and the reward has to be worth it or you might as well go and get a job and take your four weeks of holiday a year. If you're an entrepreneur, then factor in some excitement, something for you. If you spend all your time trying to keep everyone else happy, you're going to end up sad. If you're willing to take the risks involved with running your own business, you must take the rewards and factor those in as goals.

Look at it this way: if on a monthly basis you need £3k to run the business, plus £2k to run your home and associated costs and food, then your monthly target cannot be £5k. You cannot just scrape by. Your monthly target should be £7k, £8k or even £10k. Money loves a purpose so decide what you want, whether it's a motorbike, a horse or a golf club membership. Through planning, you also build motivation to succeed; and the mad thing is that if you build in the goals, you're more likely to hit them.

As an entrepreneur, you need to build a meaningful life, one that makes you happy, so work out what that looks like, what it costs and what you need to do to make it happen.

You'll start having bigger ideas – ideas that make you more efficient – and before you know it, you'll have more time to enjoy.

You don't have to be available 24/7

When you're an entrepreneur with your own business, it can be difficult to switch off. As an employee it's often easier: you go to work, you do your hours and you go home. You don't have the same emotional attachment and personal connection that you do when you own a business.

I believe that one of the big problems is that we, as business owners, have this notion that we need to be available 24/7, and that's absolutely not true. I was recently at a conference and some people were shocked when I handed them my business card and they saw that it didn't have my mobile phone number on it. They asked me how people got hold of me and I told them that, well, they don't. I have a PA system in place (which I'll talk more about later), and they can email me. Because I have had the same mobile number for years, my long-term clients know it, but now all clients come to me via the PA system which helps me better plan and safeguard my time.

However, what you have to remember is that people will often message you because they think something is urgent when, in reality, it could wait – and it definitely doesn't need to be done at 6pm on a Saturday evening.

For example, in the past, I could get a phone call or email from a client on a Saturday telling me that they desperately need their mortgage offer; should I send it to them? The answer is no. What are they going to do with it on a Saturday evening? The next step after I send their mortgage offer is for them to pass it on to their solicitor. Is the solicitor going to be working on a Saturday night? No. Do they have a mobile number for them? Of course not. How does this apply to your business? Do clients urgently seek clarity or updates that seem unreasonable or unnecessary? What makes it urgent or important to them? How can you help to reassure and educate them so your boundaries aren't constantly being tested?

The point is that, while you could argue that many of us are in a service industry and should therefore respond to clients, you have to manage their expectations. I'm not a brain surgeon. Nothing I do is a matter of life and death. That means a client can wait until Monday morning to hear from me if they get in touch over the weekend. Set your business boundaries from the outset so that everyone knows where they stand.

I have a separate work phone, which I turn off at 5pm every Friday. There's no point in being at everyone's beck and call when the other links in the chain aren't at everyone's beck and call. You need to make sure you're spending quality time with your family and loved ones, which means you can't put work first 24/7.

Upholding your boundaries

It's all well and good setting boundaries, like my decision to turn my work mobile off at 5pm on a Friday, but you have to make sure that once you set boundaries you uphold them.

I've made the mistake of letting my boundaries slip, and it's cost me. For instance, more recently I've stopped working every

Friday, but in the past I've let my guard down and answered the office phone when it rings. Usually, the response I get from my client is, "Oh, I didn't think you worked Fridays, I was just going to leave a message with your answering service." At that point, I'm quietly cursing myself for answering the phone, because my clients don't expect me to be there and I need to stick to the boundaries that I put in place.

Fundamentally this is about time protectionism: protecting your time, both when you're at work and when you're not. One of the best things that I spend money on in my business is a service called All Day PA (other virtual assistants are available). What they do is answer my phones and take messages. That means whenever someone calls my business, day or night, weekday or weekend, the phone is answered by an actual person.

They take a message and then email me, and I can then decide whether I or one of my team need to respond to that query or not. It costs me an average of £30 a month and I'd say it's a brilliant way to protect your time.

Plan your spare time

It can be incredibly easy to let spare time drift. We've all done it, where we've got to the end of the weekend and don't really know how we spent the last two days. The key to avoiding this scenario is to plan your spare time as much as you plan your work time.

When I say spare time, I'm talking about any time that you're not at work – that's evenings, weekends and holidays. This principle of planning your spare time to the same degree that you plan your work time comes from the Strategic Coach® Programme. And I'm not saying that this is necessarily an easy thing to do, but in a perfect world, you should plan something positive to do at the weekends and in the evenings.

What that is will depend on you and your partner, and your

kids if you have them. You need to make sure you're planning time with your other half. Of course, if you're single you can do whatever you want in your spare time, but if you're in a relationship and/or have a family, then you need to consider what they'll want to do too. Have a meeting with your partner and kids. Talk about what you'd all like to do and share the plan that you come up with.

I remember once hearing a story about a man whose kids would get out his golf clubs for him every Saturday morning and send him off to play golf, because if he didn't play a round of golf, he was a miserable bugger for the whole weekend. The kids worked out that when their dad played golf he was a much happier person to be with for the rest of the weekend. It was win-win for that round of golf to be part of the plan every weekend.

This book focuses on the fundamentals to support you to make your goals come true, but it's important to remember that the goals you write for your personal life and your spare time are just as important as the ones you write for your business. Never neglect them, and remember, there must always be time for beer.

Chapter 10: "If You're Going Through Hell...

... Keep going" – Winston Churchill

This is a quote that's famously attributed to Winston Churchill during the Second World War (there is no guarantee he actually said this, but the sentiment stands regardless). It stems from the idea that Hell is certainly not a place where you want to stop. But it's also about the concept that the only way to get out of whatever Hell you're experiencing is to just keep going, to keep pushing.

While it might have been said in the context of war, where there could be bullets flying past you and bombs going off, it's applicable to anyone who runs their own business too. You might not be in physical danger, but that doesn't mean you aren't under immense pressure. There are countless stories of people who hit a rough patch and just give up, only to later discover they were just metres away from that gold seam that would have changed their lives. You don't want to be one of the people who just gives in.

Why did I keep going?

This is a topic that's very close to my heart, because I've been through some very difficult times and I've come out the other side by keeping going.

In 2010, I was on the edge of bankruptcy. And now, ten years later, I'm a millionaire. All because I kept going. I'm proof that this mindset works. I established my business, DB Financial, in June 2006. In November 2006, my mum passed away, and 12 weeks later, in February 2007, my dad also died. I'd been so busy setting up my business at the start that I hadn't seen either of them as much as I would have liked to at that time. It's still one of my biggest regrets.

When my parents passed away, I received an inheritance and Bonnie and I used that to buy a bigger house. We had a big mortgage and we kept our other house and rented it to a friend. Not long after we'd moved, towards the end of 2007, the market for mortgages dried up. It was the beginning of the global financial crisis that took hold in 2008.

As I mentioned in Chapter 7, before the crash, I was arranging 15 to 20 mortgages per month, which gave me a pretty decent income. In 2008, I arranged just 25 mortgages in the whole year. This period was really scary. We had a big mortgage and other debts. We were borrowing from Peter to pay Paul and we became trapped in the debt spiral. In 2010, I decided to seek help to make our financial situation more manageable.

In the midst of all of this, it would have been very easy for me to walk away from my business. But I didn't and there were two big reasons why. Firstly, I didn't want to let Bonnie down. She had put a lot of time and energy into the business, and I wanted to make a success of it to give us both the lifestyle that we wanted.

Secondly, I wanted to make my mum proud. When I was a child, my dad had worked for the armed forces, which meant we moved around a lot. All of our moves were timed around my schooling, so that I'd have security and stability in my education at key points. I have a brother who's a year younger than me, but all of our moves were arranged for me to be able to do my O Levels and my A Levels with minimal disruption, as I was the brighter of the two of us (that's what I tell myself!).

When I was younger, my mum wanted me to be the chairman of Imperial Chemical Industries (ICI), which at that stage was the largest manufacturing company in the UK. ICI was bought out and disbanded in 2008, but when I was growing up it was one of the biggest businesses in Britain. In the 1980s, John Harvey-Jones was the chairman; he was like that generation's Peter Jones, and my mum's goal was for me to be as successful as him.

Until I set up my own business in 2006, I'd been involved in various partnerships. However, setting up DB Financial was a really big and important step for me. I wanted to make my mum proud, and so giving up just wasn't an option. Even during the most challenging times, I wouldn't have considered giving up my business. If you're going through Hell, keep going.

How did I keep going?

Having the desire to keep going is important, but that alone won't get you through tough times. I took a number of practical steps that allowed me and Bonnie to avoid bankruptcy and to keep my business going.

In 2010, I realised that I needed help to manage my debt and financial situation. I reorganised our outgoings into a more manageable monthly payment. Bonnie and I also made sacrifices to help bring in some extra money. Our house is just a short drive from Gatwick Airport, so we rented out our driveway to people who were going away. We also rented two of the rooms in our house to pilots who were training at the easyJet training centre nearby. For most of this period, we were just doing what we had to in order to make ends meet.

Renting out rooms to people we didn't know didn't always go smoothly either. I remember one woman who lived with us, we'll call her Sally, who didn't really fit in. I was the one who'd agreed for her to stay with us; and I remember one evening we had some friends round and I said that it was just typical that the one time I choose someone to move in they're an absolute nightmare, and that it doesn't happen to Bonnie, she just gets these nice charming pilots.

Anyway, I hadn't realised that Sally had come home and was sitting at the bottom of the stairs. She heard everything I said. She even tried to call me to tell me that she could hear me, but my phone was on the mantelpiece and I didn't hear it ringing. The next morning, she confronted me about it and asked me to apologise. I told her I wasn't sorry that I'd said it, but that I was sorry she'd heard. Of course, not long afterwards she moved out.

However, when Sally did move out, she kept hold of our key. I had kept £50 of her deposit to pay for the repainting of her room because she'd put posters up on the walls and the Blu-tack had ruined the paint. We had an argument over that because she said she'd come and repaint the room herself if that was the problem, and I had to explain that keeping our key wasn't the equivalent of me taking £50 to pay for some decent paint to redecorate her room. In the end, she returned the key, but that's just an example of the additional stress we went through during that time.

Having lodgers and sharing your home like that is far from ideal, and it's particularly difficult when you're already on edge because there's no money around and you're having to be careful.

Financially, we were also renting out our old house, which was generating a bit more income. However, we were renting it to a friend initially, for about £900 a month. When our friend moved out after five years and we put it up for rent on the open market, we were able to get £1,350 a month for the property. With hindsight, that extra money would have been incredibly useful and would have made a difference to us, but it was rented to a friend and well looked after. The new higher rent didn't always come in on time as we didn't really know the new tenant. This added more stress when we could have done without it.

The other thing that kept me going was having a dog that I could take out for walks. The dog really was a lifesaver because it meant we went out for walks and had a bit of distraction. Walking the dog also allowed us to meet some of our neighbours, whom we became friends with and whom we could have round for dinner, or go to their houses (which also meant we could avoid going out to restaurants and the costs involved with that). Having that sense of community also helped in those difficult times.

E + R = O

This formula is what I aspire to live by. **E**vent + **R**eaction = **O**utcome. This comes from the idea that events happen and you can't control the events. However, what you can control, in fact all you can control, is your reaction to the events. How you react to the events in your life will determine the outcome.

So, if you have a negative reaction to an event, you're more likely to get a negative outcome. If, on the other hand, you have a positive reaction to an event, you're more likely to get a positive outcome. There are no guarantees, but by reacting in a positive way, you're increasing the chances of seeing a positive outcome, and the same holds true if you react negatively.

I don't remember where I first heard about this formula, I have a feeling that I have Jack Canfield to thank for it, but it's a great approach to life, and it's one that I've carried around and tried to live by for over 20 years. Successful people focus on their reactions.

In the summer of 2021, a number of my more speculative investments had dropped by 75%, my house was severely vandalised, and my business was facing some internal staffing issues. I cannot 100% control these situations, so the question becomes how best do I react to them?

I could be angry, allow that anger to control me and spiral into a negative mindset which is more likely to create a negative outcome, impact on work and home life, and hold me back from achieving goals. That same anger isn't going to miraculously change the stock markets or get my windows fixed. It's not going to find a solution.

The only option is to find a more positive way to react and keep things in perspective, and this is important even when the negative situation has been created by you. I made a big mistake that I'll share with you in the next chapter.

Developing your inner resources

While there are practical things you can do when you're going through Hell to keep you going, like those I've discussed in this chapter and elements earlier in the book, such as budgeting and income, there are also inner resources that you need to cultivate in order to keep pushing.

You need to have confidence, resilience and a degree of arrogance. I'd say that I'm arrogant, but not in the extreme. So, I have strong opinions about things and I'm willing to change my opinion, but you need to have a very compelling argument if you're going to convince me that I'm wrong.

It's also essential to have confidence and self-belief. I'm convinced that the only person you need to believe in is yourself, you don't need to believe in anyone else. I really do think it's that simple: believe in yourself. You will take a battering along the way and you'll encounter people who don't like your attitude or what you've got to say, but provided this self-confidence comes from a place of love and the genuine belief that what you're doing is right, you'll become unstoppable.

This isn't about being single-minded and looking inward. It's about connecting with the world around you, recognising who needs you and who's around you and supporting you, and being able to tap into that part of you that allows you to act from a position of love. If you help other people and accept help from others, you create a chain that passes the good on.

Authenticity is everything

One of the most important things I've learned is that you have to be authentic in everything you do. I've also learned that if you're authentic you don't have to work so hard. If you're just being yourself it's the easiest thing in the world because you're just being who you are. You're not putting up a front or pretending to be something you're not. You're you. Having that authenticity makes everything easier.

However, it's also essential in this line of work. Fundamentally, the role of a financial adviser is to help people find the courage and give them the confidence to take care of their families. That's all we need to do. There are so many people in this line of work who try to trick people, or confuse them with charts, but that's not the way to go about it.

This integrity will help you when you're going through Hell. It's how you calibrate your internal compass, if you like. We all have gut feelings about situations and those come from our core – our integrity helps us to see opportunities. Of course, we've all done things that when we look back, we realise they really weren't a good idea. Hindsight is a wonderful thing. But the general rule is to trust your gut feeling and if something sounds too good to be true, it's not a good idea.

When you have integrity and are authentic, you attract other people who are like you. This gives you an invaluable support network when you are going through tough times.

If you establish your business because you genuinely want to help and do the right thing, you can make a fantastic amount of money without ever sacrificing your integrity, and as a result you'll have loyal clients and repeat business.

Chapter 11: My Big Mistake

Learning vs earning

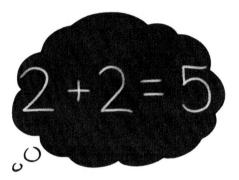

We all make mistakes but that doesn't make you a failure. It means that the strategy that you used in that situation was ineffective. You are not a failure. As an entrepreneur, you will encounter events that are within your control and sometimes you will suffer a lapse of judgement. It's inevitable.

By continuing to positively react to each situation, you are learning; even if that mistake costs you money, you are learning, and that learning will stop you repeating that mistake. It builds your resilience muscle.

What's more, trying to make everything perfect from the get-go stifles creativity and progress. Sometimes it is easier and faster to make a mistake and learn from it. In my team, I have a philosophy where a staff member can make a decision if it costs the business £200 or less. I don't need to approve every single thing. That's time-consuming. Even if they make a mistake, I'd rather they learn from it than keep coming to me to make decisions. My focus needs to be on scaling my business.

By working in this way my staff members build confidence,

resilience and knowledge. They learn how to positively respond to any negative consequences. This means when bigger mistakes happen, and they will, they are better prepared to learn than lie down defeated. I am no stranger to mistakes.

My big mistake

My business trajectory could have turned out very differently. Instead of writing this book and sharing my story with you so that you can create your version of success, I might have been peeking out from behind prison bars.

You didn't see that coming did you? And neither did I. I hadn't intentionally committed any criminal activity and nor will I ever, but I had unwittingly signed off on a perfectly presented mortgage application without reviewing the intricate detail. It was a high-pressure situation as the client was the middle purchaser in a chain and there was a lot riding on the sale going through. Long story short, the applicant was involved in mortgage fraud along with two others.

I was called to court to defend myself. I was so terrified by the thought of how this might impact my life and business that I had to stop the car to throw up.

I didn't blame myself for this mistake but I did take full responsibility for it. If you think about it, the word responsibility is response-ability. It's what you do next that counts.

It would have been very easy for me to lose confidence in my abilities and quit. I could have responded to that terrifying situation with more fear, but I didn't. I dug deep for the lesson, made some promises to myself and moved on.

If I had just been dipping a toe in the ocean, I might have been tempted to call it a day with my business; but having big goals, big dreams, keeps you focused. Remember what your vision is and why it matters to you.

Mistakes matter because you learn from them. What you cannot afford to do is dwell on them.

What helps you move beyond a mistake?

Whilst a compelling goal will pull you forward, having good, supportive people around you makes the world of difference. If you've used up the goodwill of your family and friends because you are never available to do what you've promised, your business is failing you.

When you clearly communicate your goals, your dreams and ambitions to your family and the people around you, they understand the journey you are on. They know better how to support you because they know what is at stake for you. If they don't understand your goals, if they're bitter or resentful, they'll condemn you, think you're crazy or just won't support you. You need to find your people so that when mistakes do happen, you can pick yourself up faster, dust yourself off and get back to business.

Chapter 11: My Big Mistake

Chapter 12: The Cost of Loyalty

Mercedes vs BMW

"You will get all you want in life if you help enough other people get what they want." – Zig Ziglar[1]

That quote sums up what I'm going to talk about in this chapter. I've also got a personal story that explains the cost of loyalty.

In all of my goals that I've written down, I've always said, "I drive a Mercedes." It might be this Mercedes or that Mercedes, but while the model changes over the years, the brand doesn't. But the funny thing is that I actually drive a BMW.

The reason for that is very simple. A good friend of mine, Mario, was a car salesman for BMW. I wanted to support him, so I went to his dealership and bought a BMW. Although I did this to support him, the irony is that he gave me such a good deal he didn't end up making any money on it. His sales director even asked him how much money he thought he'd

---

[1] Quoted in Brian Patrick Eha (Nov 2012) "Zig Ziglar and the Importance of Helping Others", Entrepreneur, [Online article] [Accessed on 26th Aug 2021] https://www.entrepreneur.com/article/225131

made on the sale to me. Mario guessed it was about £1,000, but it was actually just £100. By the time he'd filled up the fuel tank and thrown in a couple of other extras, he didn't make any money on that sale at all, so he just got credit for it.

That was a few years ago. More recently, I decided to swap the BMW I bought originally for a new one, because the one I had was a little bit low and uncomfortable to drive (I must be getting OLD!). This time I told Mario that, while I appreciated him getting me an amazing deal, he couldn't do that again. He had to make sure he made some money on the sale.

So, despite the fact that one of my goals is to drive a Mercedes, my last two cars have been BMWs, and that's the cost of loyalty. Sometimes you forgo the things that you want for a friend or to help someone else out.

It's not a cost, it's an investment

I call it a cost, but I do that in an ironic way. I don't really see anything as a cost, I see it as an investment. In fact, everything, one way or another, is an investment. It might be an investment for some peace of mind. It might be an investment in a nice feeling. It might be an investment in somebody else. It's a cost that you should pay, it's worthwhile; but really, if you think of it as an investment, then it ceases to be a cost at all.

Coming back to the story about me choosing a BMW over a Mercedes, it's important to remember that driving a Mercedes has been on my list of goals for years. It's something that I've visualised many times. I even had a Mercedes at one point before life became difficult financially. This goal has motivated me to work hard. But in spite of all of that, driving a BMW rather than a Mercedes is a sacrifice I've been willing to make because it fits in with my core belief in loyalty.

Remember the chapter where I talked about SMART goals? If your goal isn't SMART (specific, measurable, achievable, realistic, trackable) you change it. Even though driving a

Mercedes fits all the criteria for a SMART goal, it doesn't fit in with my beliefs around loyalty. For now, I've chosen to drive a BMW. If Mario ever moves to Mercedes, I'll have my opportunity to own a Mercedes and go back to my original goal.

How loyalty helps in business

I've talked about a few core qualities that you need in order to succeed in business, such as integrity and authenticity in Chapter 10. Loyalty is one of those core qualities too.

Loyalty leads to longevity. I can tell you that with certainty. I have clients who have been with me for 20, 25, even 30 years. The reason they're loyal to me is because I'm loyal to them. That means you need to be honest with them and have integrity in what you're saying; that breeds loyalty. What you have to remember is that what you put out into the world comes back in spades.

In the last couple of years, I have stopped offering so many face-to-face meetings and moved many of my clients to an online system where they are looked after by someone else. Of course there was always a risk that client numbers would drop, but I had already laid the foundations and taken care of the complicated stuff so the majority of them were happy to be looked after remotely, and happy for me to handle their finances in that way.

I completed all of the necessary due diligence to make sure it would be a good fit for my clients. It wasn't a difficult transition because we're loyal to each other. They trusted me and my recommendation, and for them it meant a more efficient and streamlined process at a slightly lower cost.

We sent them letters proposing the new way of working, and the transition took six to eight months to complete which was plenty of time for us to answer questions. There were some clients who simply weren't happy to use the system with no input from me, so we came to an agreement that I would have a quick phone call with them in advance and they would proceed based on that conversation. This gave them the reassurance they needed.

Build relationships with loyalty

There are plenty of examples of people who aren't loyal to their clients, but that often means their clients aren't loyal to them. You can't trust people who are fickle and who behave without integrity and loyalty.

When someone reaches out to connect with me on LinkedIn, for example, I'll always have a look to see who they are and what connections we have in common. If I accept a connection from someone and within 30 seconds I receive a message telling me what they can do for me, I've turned off. They've made it transactional. They haven't tried to build a relationship with me, or a lasting connection. They're only interested in selling and, to me, that's boring.

When you look at their profile, they'll most likely have had ten jobs in the last 15 years. A year here, a couple of years there and so on. They don't stick to anything because they get people on board and then they move on. To be fair, some people might move around so much because they're looking for the right thing. But more often than not, they're salespeople jumping from one place to another, and when I see that I always take anything they say to me with a pinch of salt.

If anyone is struggling with this, first and foremost I'd say that it means you haven't found your calling or the right fit. I'm in the protection arena of financial services – life insurance, income protection insurance and so on. I'd say that this is one of the only businesses within financial services where, if you do the right thing with care for the products you're selling and the people you're selling to, you can't sell too much. No widow has ever complained because her husband had too much life insurance.

Loyalty doesn't cost you a thing
Loyalty, like the other core internal qualities I've talked about, such as integrity, authenticity and honesty, doesn't cost you any money. But these core qualities are all invaluable tools that can help you and help the people around you.

The main point I'm making in this chapter is that you need to focus on your internal qualities first. Work on what's inside and apply those core qualities to your life. If you do that, then you'll find that the external things you're looking for – like a Mercedes – will come to you. Sometimes they might be in the form of a BMW though.

Think of that quote from Zig Ziglar at the start of this chapter: "You will get all you want in life if you help enough other people get what they want." It's as simple as that.

Chapter 13: You Fat B*stard!

Being fit for purpose

I want to start by clarifying that I'm the fat b*stard this chapter refers to. It's something that I'm working on because I know how important it is to stay healthy. If you think that you could be healthier too, then this chapter will be especially important. Even if you don't class yourself in that group, there are still some important lessons to learn about looking after yourself.

Improving my health and fitness all began when I started with the new firm in Egham nearly 20 years ago, and I was commuting there from Redhill. This was when they were widening the M25 to make it four/five lanes, so there were a lot of roadworks. That meant it could take anywhere from 45 minutes to three hours to get to work.

To avoid the traffic, I started going to work really, really early. I'd get to the office and be the only person there. Opposite the office was a gym. I decided that, rather than getting in early and starting work, I might as well pop to the gym and at least I could use their showers after a workout, and so on.

The first day I went in there, I ran about 100m on the treadmill and I was ready to throw up. I was so unfit. I spent a lot of time in the car. We lived close to a McDonald's, a chip shop, a Beefeater – it was easy to walk to these places, pick up a takeaway and eat it at home. It's easy to see why I wasn't at the peak of physical fitness.

At that time of day, I was the only person in the gym, apart from the owner, Karen, who used to train early in the morning. She helped me with my training and, 18 months later, I completed the London Marathon. I don't tell people that I ran the London Marathon, because I walked some of it, but I got my medal and that was one of the goals that was on my list.

I'd like to add that I didn't feel ready when I stepped up to the starting line. The furthest I'd run before the marathon was 15 miles, because that's all I'd had time to train for. In actual fact, I missed out on the ballot initially and felt quite relieved, only for a friend who worked for the marathon to offer me a space. I couldn't say no, so that was it, I was in, no turning back.

I found myself with the thousands of other runners, and several hours and one missing toenail later, I'd completed the course. The support you get from the crowd on the way round is really what keeps you going. If you're going to run the London Marathon, make sure you've got your name in big letters on the front and back of your shirt so people can cheer you on, it gives you a real boost (just like having good people around you in business).

My point isn't that you should go to the gym and start training for a marathon. My point is that you should get some support. It doesn't matter what the goal is, but I think you should always find that support wherever it might come from.

Now let's return to me being a fat b*stard: my support network as I try to lose weight comes from the "Gut Busters". We're three guys, all in our mid-50s, and each week we check in with our weight and BMI and, of course, there's a bit of banter along the way.

Personally, I need something to aim for and look forward to – like completing the London Marathon or trekking up Kilimanjaro. This year, we've decided we're going to complete the Three Peaks Challenge. Most of the guys who are signing up aren't particularly fit, so instead of climbing Snowdon, Scafell Pike and Ben Nevis in 24 hours, we're giving ourselves 36 hours.

Remember that your goals always need to be achievable, and if they're not you change them. That's what we've done here, by giving ourselves a little bit longer. This isn't about being the best, or the fastest, this is about giving yourself a goal that you feel you can achieve.

Why is your fitness important?

There are three main reasons why it's important to stay in shape, and especially if, like me, you're someone who deals with health, whether that's through insurance or coaching!

Firstly, when you're interacting with clients, you're trying to give them the confidence to make decisions about their future. If you're building a business, it's important that you can imagine a future where you are healthy and able to fully function; and if you want people to buy into what you do, they need to be able to see that you will be around for the foreseeable and that you're not going to drop dead any second.

To me, it seems rather ironic if you turn up to a meeting and you're overweight, out of breath, sweating, but you're there to inspire them to work with you.

Secondly, these conversations with clients revolve around their goals, their aspirations and their life. If you have poor health, chances are most of your time and resources go into managing that instead of propelling you or them towards a goal.

Finally, how you look after yourself and your immediate environment reflects on a lot of other areas of a person's life. You've got to think about how you come across to potential clients. If you take care of your health and fitness, that indicates that you take care of other aspects of your life, and therefore your client will believe that you're going to take care of them. By looking after yourself well you convey that you will, in turn, look after them well.

Remember that people tend to care more about themselves than about other people. As a result, if you don't appear to care about yourself, it might suggest you'll care less about others.

Finding time to get fit

In our profession, we spend a lot of time sitting in front of a computer, sitting in meetings with clients, and sitting in cars or on trains going to meetings with clients. If you want to lose weight and/or improve your fitness, you need to make time for it.

That means putting it in your diary. It has to be a non-negotiable part of your week. I'm the first to admit that I'm not perfect, but I'm working on it and without dedicating a bit of time to my fitness, I'd easily be obese.

Chapter 14: All You Need Is Love

Or how to go the extra mile in 100 yards

There can be a lot of expectations around love. The concept of a soul mate, the only person for you. The idea of your eyes meeting across a crowded room and instantly falling in love. I suppose that can happen. But in my experience it's more often the case that you connect with someone and then love comes, but you have to work at it.

I would say that love has played an unquestionable role in my journey to success. However, I've had to work at it. Take my marriage as an example. I have the most wonderful wife. But one of my goals has always been to be happily married to Bonnie. As I've already explained, writing goals doesn't have to be something you do every single day, but it does have to be something you do consistently. Your goals always need to be in the present tense.

Being happily married to Bonnie is a goal that I've been writing for years. And it's true. I am happily married to Bonnie. For me, there are two ways of looking at this goal. One is that it's a reminder that I am happily married, and that can be useful when you're going through a difficult time. The other way of looking at that goal is as an instruction. Remember the principle of E + R = O (Event + Reaction = Outcome)? This instruction that you're happily married can help you choose a reaction to an event. If you've told yourself that you're happily married to someone, your reaction to an event is likely to be different than if you don't feel happy in your marriage.

I'm not saying that this is easy. Long-term relationships require work. Sometimes it's hard work and sometimes it's easy work, but either way it's something that you have to constantly work at.

Relationships are 100/100

People often say that a relationship should be 50/50, but I don't think that's right. If you're only prepared to give 50%, it's never going to work. A relationship should be 100/100, you have to take 100% responsibility for your part if you want it to work.

Sometimes you'll be giving your 100% and your other half might only be giving 50%, and at other points it will be the other way around. But the point is that if you love somebody, you'll work your way towards giving 100% as often as you possibly can. Sometimes we need to remind ourselves of that, which is why having "being happily married" can be a very useful goal.

While you should always be striving to hit that 100%, you should also know that you're never going to get there because nobody is perfect. There will always be something nibbling away at it, but it's about progress not perfection.

Don't bail on love

There's no doubt about it, relationships can be hard, but that doesn't mean you should bail out of them as soon as things start to get rough. Think back to Chapter 10 and that quote: "If you're going through Hell, keep going." Relationships are the same. There will be hard times, but there will also be good times if you work at things.

My parents had their problems, but they stayed together through thick and thin. It's something that's always stuck with me. I know that there have been times in my and Bonnie's relationship when she or I could have said, "Let's call this a day." And sometimes it's understandable that you might feel that way, especially when things are rough, but you have to balance that out by remembering what attracted you to one another in the first place. I don't think you need to be soul mates to have a happy marriage and lasting relationship, but you do need to be tolerant. Nobody is perfect.

I also believe that love keeps going if you make a decision to keep it going. You have to make the effort to remain connected. If you become complacent, you can drift apart and before you know it, it becomes impossible to get back together. It really doesn't take long for a rift to open up, so love is something you have to keep working on.

How to stay connected

I can give you some practical tips on how to stay connected within a relationship. Firstly, you have to learn to bite your tongue. Secondly, write down all of the jobs that you're asked to do and make sure that you do them within six months. If you've been asked to do something three times, you should do it instantly. You might think I'm joking, but I genuinely have a list in my phone that's titled: "Jobs for a happier Bonnie."

The other thing I used to do, although I've had to stop because it winds Bonnie up, is ask which jobs are the most important, because there is only so much free time in a weekend. I don't want to have ten jobs on my list, get through eight of them but still be in the doghouse because the two I didn't do were actually the most important. I'm not a psychic, which is why it's so important to communicate.

You might think that this sounds a little trite or simplistic, but it's about making an effort and that's what love is.

It's also important to keep the romance alive. One of the best ways to do that is to go the extra mile when someone isn't expecting it. One of my top tips is to buy flowers every now and again. Don't do it every week, because then it becomes a habit and an expectation, but every now and again buy flowers. Don't just pop to your nearest garage either, go to Marks & Spencer. If you're going to make the grand gesture of buying flowers, buy quality. Spend £12 instead of £5.

Whenever I buy flowers for Bonnie, I go to Marks & Spencer. It's two miles away and it's not on my way home from the office, but I always go there to buy flowers. I don't just pop into the garage that's walking distance from my office. It takes a little extra effort and it makes all the difference. You just have to give your 100% with no expectation of getting 100% back.

As I was writing this book, someone mentioned a book by Gary Chapman called The Five Love Languages – turns out you could spend 25 years in a relationship speaking the wrong "love language", or not spending quite enough time using the right one. You really do not want to do that...

According to Chapman, the five ways to express and experience these so-called "love languages" are:

- Words of affirmation
- Quality time
- Giving gifts
- Acts of service
- Physical touch

If you have the feeling that you are not quite on the same wavelength with your spouse/significant other, check out this book. There is a good chance that you are speaking in your love language (how you would like to be treated) and your spouse is speaking to you in theirs, and it is not quite compatible. Worth a look and it will go some way to you achieving your 100%.

Why do I do things out of love?

As I said earlier in the book, there are two people whom I do things for: Bonnie and my mum. I still do things for the love of my mum because it helps me to keep her alive. I learned a lot from her, my qualities like honesty, integrity and patience all came from her. She also taught me that you should just be yourself, you shouldn't be different people. Be you and you can't go far wrong.

I do things for the love of Bonnie because she honestly has no idea how great she is. She is so much more capable than she gives herself credit for. She struggles to believe in herself and she worries an awful lot about what other people think, but everyone who meets her loves her. Bonnie had a really hard upbringing, and she came out the other side. She so much deserves to be loved. It's no more or less than she deserves. While she infuriates me sometimes, and I'm sure I infuriate her, I always love her. I sometimes think that if I could give her a little bit of my belief in her, she'd be even more incredible. I think I need to tell her that sometimes.

Helping others is an extension of love

For me, doing things from a place of love makes a positive difference to other people's lives. When I talk about helping other people, it doesn't always have to be a grand gesture. For example, I'm the kind of person who will collect up all of the glasses on our table and put them back on the bar before I leave a pub. There's no harm in it and it's only a small gesture, but these little things make a difference. Often I think that surely everybody behaves like this, but then I realise that they don't. And that's why making those small gestures does make a difference.

Let me give you an example. I was at a four-day conference

(MDRT) in America in 2019. On the first day, I queued up with everyone else for coffee. When I got to the front of the queue, I started chatting to the barista while she made my coffee, and she told me during this chat that she had a son. I had a couple of tiny koalas attached to my badge so I gave her one of them for her son. The following day I was in the same queue and when I got to the front the same barista served me. Her face lit up when she saw me, considerably more than it had for the 20–30 people she'd served ahead of me. There were 14,000 people at that conference. She greeted me with a smile and said, "Hi, how are you today?" I responded, "I'm great but how do you possibly remember me from yesterday?" She told me it was not only because I'd given her the koala for her son, but also because I was one of the only people she'd served who said please and thank you. I was flabbergasted.

I have another example from later at that same conference. I was in the hotel bar area when I heard the young waitress nearby give out a bit of a sigh. I asked if she was having a tough day and she turned to me and admitted that she was in the middle of a double shift and was feeling the strain. I told her that she was doing an amazing job (she was) and left her a tip to say thanks.. It visibly lifted her spirits. Later that evening, I was looking for a nice glass of red wine at the bar, but as it wasn't the hotel I was staying in, I was struggling to get served at that time of the evening as I had no cash and no room key. The waitress I'd seen earlier in the day spotted me and brought over the largest glass of red wine I've ever seen, at no charge. I think it's safe to say she wouldn't have done that had I not paid her a very simple compliment earlier in the day.

How does all of this relate to you being an entrepreneur?

When you are you, more of you shines through – and you are the unique selling point of your business. People buy people, they don't buy some one dimensional idea. They are investing in you, your beliefs, your passion, your drive, your vision, who and how you are. Work on developing your kindness, loyalty, integrity, moral fibre, resilience, doing the right thing and you'll go far.

Chapter 14: All You Need Is Love

Conclusion

You have a lifetime of business wisdom in just one book, what do you plan to do with it? These are the key takeaways from the book, use them as a gentle reminder:

- Start by dealing with the simple things and taking slow and steady steps.
- Always trust your gut. If something just doesn't feel right then don't do it.
- Live with integrity. It's one of your most valuable qualities.
- Be yourself. People will love and trust you for it.
- Believe in yourself. Sometimes it's the hardest thing in the world, but trust that by believing in yourself you'll find the strength and courage to achieve what you're aiming for.
- Put as much focus on your personal life as your professional life. Without meaning or reward, your determination will dwindle.
- You are always earning or learning. Mistakes can teach you and build resilience. Don't waste precious time trying to avoid them. Make progress not perfection.
- Surround yourself with good people. People who can lead you forward and people who will help you up when you're down.
- Keep reviewing your progress and taking your goals to the next level.
- If you are in a relationship, it needs to be 100/100. Going 50/50 just doesn't cut it.
- If you are married – remember Winston and keep going!!!

On the next page is your first goals list. Write down at least ten goals and don't forget to write them in the present tense, for example: "I earn ....", "I drive ....", "I am happily....", "I own....", "I turn up 15 minutes before every appointment."

If you let me have your address, I will send you your own Goals notepad, or you can pop to your local stationery store and pick one up. It will be the best investment you have ever made. Write your goals down. The next day, write them down again without referring to the ones written previously. Do this again the next day, and the next. The really important goals, just like cream, will rise to the top.

Have a really super life, I hope all your goals do come true!

Your Goals List

1.

2.

3.

4.

5.

6.

7.

8.

9.

10.

The fact that you have read all the way to the end of this book and completed your goal list tells me that you are committed to the entrepreneurial journey. Now take a photo of your list and email it to doug@dougbennett.co.uk and I will hold you to account or provide additional resources to help you achieve your goals.

For more help on how to achieve the your business goals please feel free to reach out to me and book a call by scanning the QR code to my website below:

Recommended Reading

There is amazing, exciting and inspiring information in the book titles I've shared below. Some are old-school classics, but still pertinent to modern times. It makes no sense to reinvent the wheel, so turn off the trash on TV, dive deep into these resources, feed your brain, and reap the rewards as you watch your life and business grow.

1) *The Infinite Game: How Great Businesses Achieve Long-Lasting Success* - Simon Sinek

   Sinek helps us differentiate between the finite and infinite game. A game of football is finite. It has a start and an end point. In business, you want to play the infinite game by forgetting about a quick sprint; put the basics in place and keep building.

2) *Eat That Frog* - Brian Tracy

   We all have things on our to-do lists that cause us to procrastinate. *Eat That Frog* encourages you to do the one job you want to do the least first (like eat a frog), which will encourage you to keep going so that you get to do the jobs that you love too (and you achieve more!).

3) *The One Thing: The Surprisingly Simple Truth Behind Extraordinary Results* - Gary Keller

   What is the one task that will take you forward and build momentum? Do that thing; and if you keep doing one of these things every day, it will take you further faster.

4) *Open With a Close: The Twelve-Point Guide to Closing More Sales* - Matthew Elwell

Closing a deal is the most important aspect of the process: seed the idea, build on it, sell the benefits and when it comes to the final decision, getting a yes should be the easiest part.

5) *Think & Grow Rich* - Napoleon Hill

An inspirational and motivational classic that stands the test of time when it comes to wealth philosophy. Hill walks you through the roadmap of countless historical figures and the thinking that they used to achieve extraordinary wealth. Master the secrets Hill shares (hint: it all starts in your mind).

6) *The Magic of Thinking Big* - David J Schwartz

Thinking and behaving differently create above average results. Schwartz takes you through easy-to-understand advice and strategies leading you to a fuller, happier life.

7) *The E Myth Revisited* - Michael E Gerber

The E stands for entrepreneur. Gerber dispels some of the myths around starting your own business. This book will help you learn how to grow your business in a productive way.

8) *The Power of Ambition: Unleashing the Conquering Drive* - Jim Rohn

Simple, incredible ideas from an inspiring man I was lucky enough to see once in person. Pursuing your ambition is important; Rohn rules out the notion that ambition has to be ruthless or selfish.

9) *The Richest Man in Babylon* - George S Clason

A short and interesting set of parables exploring how to overcome personal financial problems, the principles behind money, and how to create and build on wealth.

10) *How to Master the Art of Selling* - Tom Hopkins

Your whole life involves selling. It's not a dirty word, but to do it well you need to make it as nice an experience as possible. Hopkins shares practical how-to and effective selling skills that he's personally tried and tested.

11) *Traction: Get a Grip on Your Business* - Gino Wickman

Learn simple and powerful ways to run your business. This is an in-depth how-to guide to overcoming common frustrations so you can build traction with more focus and enjoyment.

12) *The 7 Habits of Highly Effective People* - Dr Stephen Covey

This is an inspiring book with so much to share. There are two habits Covey explains that really stick out for me: "start with the end in mind" and "sharpen the saw". See which of the other five are most meaningful to you.

13) *Start With Why* - Simon Sinek

I've shared two of Sinek's books because they're amazing. This takes you on a journey into how you can make your business better, and that boils down to why you do what you do. Find your why, use it to inspire others, and watch it build your business.

14) *The Gap and the Gain* - Dan Sullivan

You can have two equally successful people, same net worth, same drive, same capabilities. One of them will be happy, one will be miserable. Measuring success based on where you've come from or how far you still have to go brings instant happiness or postpones it to some time in the future. This is an excellent recipe for personal happiness when you realise that how and what you think is the deciding factor.

15) *I Am Pilgrim* - Terry Hayes

An intricate and compelling forensic criminal thriller (fiction) that I couldn't put down. When you want to step aside from the learning but still feed your mind with something clever and imaginative, I Am Pilgrim is an excellent choice!

16) *Dirty Goals: Breaking Conventional Rules to Achieve Your Dreams* - Alyn Mitlyng

Have you ever got to the end of a book about your (new) business and goal setting and you have no idea where to start? This great book by Alyn is your place to go, debunking one or two myths around goal setting to give you a clear path to getting started.

About the Author

Doug Bennett is happily married to his wife Bonnie and has two amazing sons, Jason and Jake.

Doug has been in financial services for nearly 40 years, starting out with the Halifax in the early 1980s, before engaging in a number of partnerships over the years. It was in 2006 that he decided the only person he could rely on was himself, and he set up DB Financial with his wife as an administrator.

In late 2019 he sold a proportion of his wealth planning business for a significant sum of money, which has enabled him to complete a number of his goals. It also gave him time to write his first book, Goals DO Come True, which he has now updated in this new edition aimed at small business owners, Think Simple Win Big. Doug has spoken at a number of conferences globally and plans to share his message to a much larger audience now he has more time available.

Doug is Chair of the Board of Trustees for a small local charity, Us in a Bus, for which he has previously raised funds by running a half marathon and trekking up Kilimanjaro. He now sits on the board helping to direct the charity in its efforts to connect with severely handicapped and autistic adults.

Having had a couple of financial near misses during his life, as well as meandering through financial crises in the early 1990s and the global financial crash in 2008, Doug has developed a very pragmatic attitude to life, has a wickedly dry sense of humour, and will help anyone.

More than a couple of people have said he is a lovely guy, so it must be true!

Printed in Great Britain
by Amazon